WHAT'S

WRONG

WITH

PROTECTIONISM?

WHAT'S

WRONG

WITH

PROTECTIONISM?

ANSWERING COMMON OBJECTIONS
TO FREE TRADE

PIERRE LEMIEUX

ROWMAN &
LITTLEFIELD

Lanham • Boulder • New York • London

Published in partnership with the Mercatus Center at
George Mason University

Published by Rowman & Littlefield
A wholly owned subsidiary of The Rowman & Littlefield
Publishing Group, Inc.
4501 Forbes Boulevard, Suite 200, Lanham, Maryland 20706
www.rowman.com

Unit A, Whitacre Mews, 26-34 Stannary Street, London SE11 4AB

British Library Cataloguing in Publication Information Available

978-1-5381-2211-2 cloth
978-1-5381-2212-9 paperback
978-1-5381-2213-6 ebook

Library of Congress Cataloging-in-Publication Data has been requested.

♾™ The paper used in this publication meets the minimum requirements
of American National Standard for Information Sciences—Permanence of
Paper for Printed Library Materials, ANSI/NISO Z39.48-1992.

Printed in the United States of America

Contents

Foreword
by *Donald J. Boudreaux and Daniel Griswold*   ix

Introduction   1

1. Objection: Americans Cannot Compete
   against Low-Cost Foreign Producers   7
   Essay 1: Comparative Advantage and Supply Chains   17

2. Objection: Free Trade Harms the United States   21
   Essay 2: Imports Are Not *a Deduction from GDP*   29

3. Objection: The Trade Deficit Is Bad   31
   Essay 3: The Balance of Trade   39

4. Objection: The United States Is Losing
   Its Factories   45
   *Essay 4: The New Manufacturing and the
   American Economy*   49

5. Objection: Trade Destroys Jobs   53
   Essay 5: Jobs, Jobs, Jobs, and Economic Growth   63

6. Objection: Trade Lowers Wages   69
   Essay 6: Labor Productivity and Remuneration   73

7. The Politics of Trade and a Bit More Economics   77
    Essay 7: Free Trade Agreements and NAFTA   83

8. Objection: Free Trade Is Not Fair   89
    *Essay 8: American Consumers Benefit from Trade
    with China*   95

    Conclusion   99
    Notes   103
    Index   117
    About the Author   125

Balance of trade is against us in almost every country in Europe, because those countries who rival us in manufacture and commerce by living cheaper and paying lower wages, undersell us in most foreign markets.

John Powell, English mercantilist, 1772

Foreword

Donald J. Boudreaux and Daniel Griswold

After more than seven decades of bipartisan commitment to trade liberalization, the US economy today is arguably more open to world trade and investment than at any other time in our history. Yet the policies that brought about that historic opening are being questioned by our political leaders at the highest levels. Almost daily, the news carries stories of threats of our own government to impose tariffs, terminate free trade agreements, and punish US companies for "shipping jobs overseas."

In *What's Wrong with Protectionism?*, Pierre Lemieux has written an essential book for our time and for decades to come. This book draws on more than two centuries of economic thinking and experience while marshaling the most current data and examples to illuminate the key trade issues of today, such as the trade deficit, free trade versus "fair" trade, and manufacturing in a global economy.

Americans who are concerned about the future of our economy and our place in the world should keep a copy of this book by their side whenever they watch TV or read a newspaper or scan their Twitter feed. Lemieux's work is an antidote to the misunderstandings about trade that prevail in our public discourse.

Like a skillful attorney defending an innocent client, Lemieux states the prosecution's case and then demolishes it before the jury with facts, arguments, and illustrations. His book systematically and fairly addresses the most common criticisms we hear today from those who want to curb the freedom of Americans to engage in international commerce for mutual benefit.

Among the more common criticisms of trade is the story, told by certain political leaders and pundits, that imports subtract from the US gross domestic product and that the trade deficit is a drag on growth.

Lemieux drives a stake into heart of the argument that we can boost economic growth by reducing imports and ending the trade deficit. Imports, by definition, are not part of gross domestic product, since they are produced outside the country. Imports are subtracted from the final calculation of GDP merely because they were already counted as part of total consumption, investment, and government expenditures, but then they must be removed to make sure that something not included in GDP is not counted.

Contrary to what we are told, imports are a blessing to millions of American consumers and businesses. Imports benefit domestic producers that rely on global supply chains for raw materials, components, and capital machinery in order to compete in global markets.

Lemieux shows that the trade deficit is driven by a surplus of investment capital flowing into the United States. Far from being a symbol of failure and decline, this perennial investment surplus is actually a positive sign of the relative health of the US economy. "The American current-account deficit is in large part a reflection of the fact that foreigners want to invest in America," Lemieux writes, adding, "the current-account deficit is not a cause of American decline but, on the contrary, a consequence of America's growth and attractiveness to investors."

We are told by certain political leaders and pundits that free trade must be fair trade. Here again Lemieux patiently defines the terms of the argument to show that there is nothing unfair about allowing producers to compete across international borders to deliver better products at lower prices to consumers. What is unfair is government protection of a small minority of domestic industries at the expense of millions of consumers:

> free trade is fair trade. The fair trade argument is usually an excuse for special interests or for state power. What is fair is to let each individual or private entity reach its own bargains. Even if domestic protectionism can favor some people in their own countries at the cost of harming foreigners, and especially poorer foreigners, it does not seem morally acceptable.

We are told by certain political leaders and pundits that America is losing its manufacturing base. Drawing on the most current data and research, Lemieux shows that jobs have disappeared in manufacturing not because we are making less stuff, but because we are making more advanced products more efficiently.

Americans have retained their comparative advantage in making more technologically sophisticated products, while lower-wage countries such as China produce more labor-intensive, low-tech goods such as shoes, clothing, and furniture. Meanwhile, supply chains have allowed workers in different nations to divide up tasks, with Americans supplying the higher-end components, software, and intellectual property for products assembled by workers in less-developed countries.

The predictable result of free trade is that Americans are producing more of those goods that play to our comparative advantage, while producing fewer goods that play to the advantages of other, less-developed countries. While US manufacturing companies have migrated up the value chain, they have also become more productive, producing more value-added with fewer man hours. Critics of trade lament the decline in the number of manufacturing workers while ignoring the long-term rise in real manufacturing output. Lemieux rightly concludes, "American manufacturing has 'declined' mainly in the sense that it has become more productive."

In a related argument, we are told trade destroys more jobs than it creates. Again, with a combination of argument and evidence, Lemieux demonstrates that trade is not about the number of jobs, but about the quality of the jobs available to American workers.

There is no evidence that trade reduces the total number of jobs in the economy. In fact, the number of jobs has grown over the decades in line with the working-age population. Trade does contribute to "churn" in the labor market, but the greatest source of job displacement by far is technology. As Lemieux notes, "Trade may resemble technological progress, which eliminates jobs in some sectors but creates an equivalent or higher number of jobs elsewhere in the economy."

As well as creating new and better jobs, trade delivers more choices, quality, and affordable prices for workers as they spend their paychecks. Lower prices are especially important to low-income households, because, as Lemieux explains, "People with lower budgets spend proportionately more on internationally traded goods such as manufactured goods and agricultural goods." For a working-class single mother shopping at a big-box retail supercenter, free trade is one of her best friends.

We are told by the same political leaders and pundits that the North American Free Trade Agreement (NAFTA) and other trade deals the US government has signed are "one-sided" and "disasters" that must be overhauled or terminated. While these agreements are not always perfectly executed and they typically contain compromises, they have generally restrained governments so that their citizens can enjoy greater freedom to engage in mutually beneficial trade across international borders.

As Lemieux wisely notes,

> The rules of the World Trade Organization and those of specific free trade agreements like NAFTA are useful as ways to tie the hands of national governments and avoid trade wars, which benefit no one. Ulysses asked to be tied to his ship's mast in order to resist the temptation of the sirens. The WTO and free trade agreements can be seen as means to similarly render a national government incapable of yielding to the appeal of domestic rent-seekers and the sirens of protectionism.

Not only is the economic case for free trade far stronger than the economic case for protectionism, the ethical case for free trade is also far stronger than the ethical case for protectionism. Like the economics of protectionism, the ethics of protectionism are incoherent—a fact made clear by the economic understanding so ably conveyed by Lemieux's book.

Suppose, for example, that an American—call him Smith—spends some of his income on purchases of foreign-grown sugar. In the United States, Smith must effectively pay a hefty fine, in the form of a tariff, for doing so—a fine that Smith would not have to pay were there no tariff on sugar imported into the U.S. Because Smith pays a fine to government agents if he buys foreign-grown sugar, the implication is that Smith's use of his income to buy foreign-grown sugar is ethically wrong. (This fine, of course—this tariff—also raises the price of domestically produced sugar up to that of the world price of imported sugar plus the tariff.) Smith is presumed to harm others whenever he buys foreign-grown sugar. And because the purpose of inflicting this punishment on Smith is to persuade him to instead buy American-grown sugar, the specific ethical offense that Smith is presumed to commit when he buys imported sugar is that his actions cause American sugar growers to suffer a fall in profits and some workers on American sugar farms to suffer losses of jobs. Protectionists insist, in effect, that import barriers are ethically justified in order to prevent domestic consumers from making economic decisions that, although peaceful, inflict economic harm on certain domestic producers.

Now change the example in just one small way. Suppose that Smith chooses not to buy foreign-grown sugar but, rather, to go on a strict no-sugar diet. In this case the reduction in Smith's expenditures on American-grown sugar is exactly the same as is the reduction in Smith's expenditures on American-grown sugar when he buys foreign-grown sugar. Yet the US government penalizes Smith only in the latter case (when he buys foreign-grown sugar) and not in the former case (when he switches to a diet free of sugar).

This differential treatment of Smith's different reasons for buying less American-grown sugar reveals protectionism's ethical incoherence. If it is truly wrong for Smith to conduct his economic affairs in ways that reduce the profits of particular domestic producers and destroy the jobs of particular fellow citizens—so wrong that the use of government force is justified to prevent the commission of this wrongdoing—then the details of how Smith inflicts this wrong on his fellow citizens should be irrelevant. If Smith's purchase of imported sugar is wrong because it harms domestic sugar producers, then it is also wrong for Smith to go on a sugar-free diet.

Yet very few Americans would agree with this last claim. Very few Americans would tolerate the government penalizing Smith for going on a diet. Most Americans understand that Smith is ethically entitled to conduct his dietary affairs as he likes, as long as he does so peacefully and with his own resources. The results—lower profits and fewer jobs in domestic sugar production—are no reason to penalize dieting.

As Lemieux's monograph makes clear, however, the economic effects of increased importing differ in no relevant way from those of increased dieting. In each case, resources are shifted from less-desired (or less-productive) uses into more-desired (or more-productive) uses. In each case, some jobs are destroyed while others are created. (The money that Smith saves by not buying sugar is spent or invested by Smith in other ways, all of which support other businesses and jobs.) In each case, producers' activities are justified only insofar as they satisfy the demands of consumers. And, therefore, if Smith by right should be left free to improve his life by changing his eating habits in the ways that he deems best, even when doing so inflicts some economic hardship on some fellow citizens, Smith by right should be left free to improve his life by changing his spending habits in ways that he deems best, even when doing so inflicts some economic hardship on some fellow citizens.

Protectionists will nevertheless protest that the two cases—importing and dieting—differ from each other. But the burden ought to be on protectionists to explain why. The burden ought to be on protectionists to successfully identify at least one relevant difference that justifies government intervention in the case of fellow citizens choosing to import but not in the case of fellow citizens choosing to diet (or to otherwise change the details of their economic activities). Lemieux's book shows why it is impossible for protectionists to meet this burden.

Now, more than ever, we need to remind ourselves of the economic as well as the ethical reasons why our nation has pursued a path of trade liberalization since the end of World War II. Pierre Lemieux's book is just the timely and pithy reminder that we need at this historic moment.

Introduction

Fears about free trade are widespread, both in the United States and across the world. The fears expressed in America fit into seven broad categories of objections to free trade:

- We cannot compete against low-cost foreign producers, such as workers who are paid a fraction of the wages that are prevalent in the United States.
- Free trade harms the United States.
- Free trade brings detrimental trade deficits.
- We are losing our factories.
- Free trade destroys jobs.
- Free trade lowers wages.
- Free trade is not fair, because the playing field is not level.

These fears have a long intellectual history, many dating from the rise of mercantilist thinking in 16th century Europe.[1] Promoted by businessmen and state rulers, mercantilism was similar to today's protectionism in that it tried to maximize exports and minimize imports—that is, to achieve a positive balance of trade.

The vast majority of economists, on the contrary, favor free trade. It is arguably the topic on which they are most in agreement. Since the 18th century, free-market economists have argued for free international trade. Even economists thought to be on the

Left generally oppose protectionism. For example, *New York Times* columnist Paul Krugman, the well-known winner of the 2008 Nobel Prize in economics, is a coauthor of a leading textbook on international trade that broadly defends free trade.[2] Krugman and his coauthors summarize the case for free trade (which they describe as "the standard view of most international economists") by arguing that the costs of deviating from free trade are large, and that any attempt to make exceptions to free trade will be exaggerated by the political process.[3] Economics professor Daniel Klein and his colleagues surveyed economics professors in 2010 and found that while only 16 percent of them could be characterized as "firm supporters of the principles of free enterprise" (and only 6 percent identified as Libertarian voters), 68 percent said they "oppose strongly" the policy of "tighter restrictions (e.g., tariffs and quotas) on imported goods," and 20 percent more said they "oppose [the policy], not strongly," for a total of 88 percent opposed—the largest consensus on any policy issue included in the survey.[4]

How does economics answer the common objections to free trade? The first six objections listed above are discussed in the first six chapters of this book. In chapter 7, I examine the politics of trade as well as the relationship between international trade and domestic trade. Chapter 8 then addresses the fairness objection. Finally, the conclusion pulls all these threads together. The book deals mainly with the theory of free trade, but it also provides several examples and statistics, which are mainly collected in the essays following each chapter. After reading this book, many other examples encountered in the media and in political debates should be easier to understand.

What Is Free Trade?

Free trade is generally understood to mean unhindered exchanges between individuals over political borders. It is the international (or interregional) equivalent of domestic free markets. Under free trade, any individual or private entity can make deals, as opposed to the government's making one deal for everybody—a deal that may be good for some and bad for others. Between the white and black worlds of free trade and trade prohibition, there are many degrees of gray in trade restrictions. These restrictions, imposed by political authorities, include import tariffs (also called *duties*) and nontariff barriers such as import quotas (which may be "voluntary" or overtly compulsory) or special requirements imposed on imports from some or all foreign countries. The rules of the World Trade Organization (WTO), as well as those of so-called *free trade agreements*—such as the North American Free Trade Agreement (NAFTA) or the previously envisioned Trans-Pacific Partnership—are partly about free trade, partly about harmonizing regulation.[5]

The average US tariff is less than 5 percent but the actual tariff level varies widely among goods.[6] The 3,707-page *Harmonized Tariff Schedule of the United States (2017)—Revision 1* contains the detailed rates on thousands of different products and varieties thereof. To give a few examples, automobiles face a tariff of 2.5 percent, bicycles of up to 11 percent, fishing rods of 6 percent, leather gloves of up to 14 percent, dishwashers of 2.4 percent.[7] Besides regular tariffs, special duties are imposed against alleged dumping or foreign subsidization: for example, cold-rolled steel from China is hit by a 522 percent tariff.[8] A limited number of goods and services are protected by prohibitions (for example, the 1920 Jones Act prohibits maritime cabotage by foreign ships) or by special tariffs or quotas. Imports of sugar are restricted by an import quota that, by reducing supply on the American market, increases domestic raw sugar prices by 52 percent relative to the world market (in 2016).[9]

For its opponents, free trade evokes imports entering the country. For many of its proponents, it evokes exports sold to foreign countries. This book will mainly use the opponents' concept—that is, it will emphasize the freedom to import. There are at least two reasons to do this. First, taking free trade as the freedom to import makes for a more operational concept. Because the freedom to buy internationally (to import) depends mainly on one's own government while the freedom to sell internationally (to export) depends on other governments allowing their residents to import, the former is easier to implement: it is a matter of domestic policy. Individuals presumably exert more direct influence on their own government than on foreign governments. Second, a long analytical tradition in economics, going back to Adam Smith and 19th-century economists, sees free trade mainly in terms of consumers' freedom to import.

The general question in this book then becomes, Do any of the seven common objections to free trade listed above justify limiting the freedom of Americans—either individuals or their intermediaries, such as retail stores or e-commerce sites—to import goods and services into the country?[10]

How to Read This Book

Each chapter in this book is followed by an essay. Half of these essays (essays 1, 3, 4, and 5) complement the preceding chapter with further information, including figures or tables. The other essays provide supplementary arguments and illustrations. Here is a map of the book:

1. At the end of chapter 1, which discusses the objection that Americans cannot compete against foreign producers with low labor costs, essay 1 summarizes the theory of comparative advantage (explained in the chapter), applies it to the American economy, and explains how international trade has generated complex supply chains.

2. After chapter 2, which discusses the objection that free trade somehow harms the United States, essay 2 introduces the reader to the objection—often encountered in the press—that imports are a deduction from GDP.

3. After chapter 3, which evaluates the related claim that the trade deficit is a problem, essay 3 provides background information and data on the US balance of payments and its evolution over time.

4. After chapter 4, which analyzes the objection that the United States is losing its factories, essay 4 provides data on manufacturing employment, total employment, GDP per capita as a better approximation of welfare, and the neglected growth of American manufacturing.

5. After chapter 5, which discusses the idea that trade destroys jobs, essay 5 emphasizes the important point that protectionism, not trade, destroys jobs. Trade fosters economic growth and increases the real incomes of consumers, including poorer consumers.

6. After chapter 6, which addresses the objection that trade lowers wages, essay 6 emphasizes how wages follow labor productivity and explains that, since trade boosts productivity, it also increases wages. Essay 6 also looks at the current polarization of the labor market.

7. Chapter 7, which provides a summary of the economic analysis of politics as it applies to international trade, is followed by essay 7, which discusses free trade agreements (and especially NAFTA) in light of the discussions in earlier chapters.

8. Chapter 8, which discusses the objection that trade is not fair, is followed by essay 8, which presents China as a case study in international trade, suggesting that American consumers benefit from trade with China even if they spend only a tiny part of their total budget on Chinese goods.

Hurried readers could read only the essays, but readers with more time should find that the theory and other information presented in the main text help them better understand the contents of the essays, the objections to free trade, and the world in which we live.

CHAPTER 1

Objection: Americans Cannot Compete against Low-Cost Foreign Producers

The first common objection to free trade is that low-cost producers—those that pay (or earn) low wages in countries such as China, Vietnam, Thailand, and Mexico—will always outcompete high-cost American producers. (Note that "producer" in standard economic terminology includes firms, their employees, and the self-employed.) At first, the objection seems to make sense: How can an American producer compete with foreign businesses that pay their workers a fraction of salaries in the United States? In the sweatshops of developing countries, salaries are often less than $15 a day. In places such as Vietnam or Thailand they are around $5 a day, and in extreme cases, such as in Bangladesh, salaries are a little more than $2 a day (for long workdays).[1] In Mexico, the average manufacturing wage was $4.50 an hour in 2014.[2]

This objection is not new. It was stated succinctly in 1772 by a British mercantilist author (quoted in the epigraph of this book): "Balance of trade is against us in almost every country in Europe, because those countries who rival us in manufacture and commerce by living cheaper and paying lower wages, undersell us in most foreign markets."[3] This author was actually a bit behind the times: Adam Smith's famous 1776 book, *An Inquiry into the Nature and Causes of the Wealth of Nations*, was about to demolish the mercantilist doctrine.[4] The complete answer to low-cost competition objection, however, was provided in the 19th century by David Ricardo's theory of comparative advantage.[5]

Absolute and Comparative Advantage

Consider two hypothetical countries, H (home) and F (foreign). Let's say country H is more productive and competitive in good or service h and country F is more productive and competitive in good or service f. It is easy to grasp why it is in H's interest to export h and import f, and vice versa for F. (What is a country's interest is not clear when its inhabitants have different interests, but this complication need not be addressed here. We'll see later what it implies.) Such trade will obviously make each country better off, because each produces what it can produce at lower cost and imports what others produce at lower cost. But what happens if one of the two countries is more productive in all goods—that is, what if it has what is called an *absolute advantage?* For instance, America is certainly more productive than Bangladesh at manufacturing both clothing and machinery. In that case, is trade still in the interest of both countries? The answer is generally yes.

Consider the problem at the level of the individual. An individual's best interest is to specialize in what he is best at doing and to purchase whatever else he needs from individuals who are best at producing those other things. Consider two individuals: Alex, who happens to be an accountant, and Mark, who happens to be a mechanic. Assume also that Alex is better than Mark at doing both accounting and car repairs—better in the sense that any task related to either activity would take him less time than it would take Mark. This is, of course, equivalent to saying that

Mark is worse at both callings. By assumption, then, Alex has an absolute advantage in both activities. But it may be the case—in fact, it will typically be the case—that one of the two individuals is comparatively better at one activity than at the other. Let's say that Alex is "more better" at accounting, and Mark is "less worse" at car repairs. Indeed, this is presumably why Alex has chosen accounting as his trade, and why Mark has become a mechanic. By spending his time doing accounting rather than car repairs, Alex earns more money per hour than he would save by doing his own car repairs. Conversely, Mark earns more money per hour doing car repairs than he would save by spending some of his time to do the accounting for his business.[6]

Look more carefully at what happens. When I say that the accountant is "more better" at accounting, I mean that doing accounting obliges him to sacrifice less in terms of the car repairs he could do—less than the mechanic would himself have to sacrifice in car repairs in order to do accounting. Alex does accounting at lower internal cost to himself than Mark. Similarly, when I say that Mark is "less worse" at doing car repairs, I mean that this activity costs him less in terms of the accounting output forgone—less than the accountant would himself have to sacrifice in accounting output if he were to do car repairs instead. Mark does car repairs at a lower internal cost to himself than Alex. Each one is comparatively better at doing a different activity. Each one sacrifices less of the other activity by doing what he is more efficient at doing than by doing what he is less efficient at doing. You should not waste your time doing what you do worst, and that is true even if somebody else does what you do best even better than you do. Note that there is a double comparison involved in *comparative advantage:* we compare the internal costs of two activities between two individuals. Even if one individual is less good at both tasks, each has an advantage in specializing as long as both face different internal costs.

The Theory of Comparative Advantage

The same reasoning is valid for countries. The theory or "law" of comparative advantage states that a country gains by exporting what it has a comparative advantage in producing and by importing what foreign countries have a comparative advantage in producing. For example, trade is beneficial for both the United States and Bangladesh even if the former country has an absolute advantage in every sort of production.[7]

Saying that the United States has an absolute advantage over Bangladesh in clothing and machinery means that its factors of production (labor, physical capital, land) can produce more of either machinery or clothes than can Bangladesh's. Comparative advantage, on the other hand, refers to the fact that the United States' advantage is stronger in machinery than in clothing. On its side, Bangladesh has less of a disadvantage in producing clothes than it has in producing machinery; this is equivalent to saying that Bangladesh has a comparative advantage in producing clothes.

We can look at this from a slightly different angle. The United States can produce more machinery than Bangladesh by sacrificing a given volume of clothing production, and Bangladesh can produce more clothing than the United States by sacrificing a given volume of machinery production. "More than" means at a lower cost—that is, by sacrificing less of the other good. In other words, the United States can transform clothing into machinery (by using resources to manufacture the latter instead of the former) at a lower cost than Bangladesh can; and Bangladesh can transform machinery into clothing (by using resources to manufacture the latter instead of the former) at a lower cost than the United States can. The comparative advantage comes from the fact that the *internal* costs of producing the two goods are comparatively different between the two countries. This amounts to saying that, as far as production capabilities are concerned, the United States is comparatively "more better" at producing machinery, and Bangladesh is comparatively "less worse" at producing clothing.

Of course, if both countries produced only clothes, more would be produced in the United States, and the same is true for machinery: this is because of the United States' absolute advantage. But the United States has to sacrifice more clothes than Bangladesh does to produce a given volume of machinery, while Bangladesh must sacrifice more machinery than the United States to produce a given quantity of clothes: this describes the comparative advantage of each country.

If, under these conditions, the United States specializes in machinery and exports part of its machinery production to Bangladesh, it can obtain for those exports more clothes than could have been produced domestically. Bangladesh is in the opposite position: if it specializes in clothing and exports part of its production, it can obtain in exchange more machinery than it could have produced. Specializing in one field of production means moving resources (such as labor and computers) from the other field of production. By specializing in the production of the good for which it has a comparative advantage and by importing the other good, each country obtains a greater quantity of at least one good than if it had produced both goods for itself.

We can express this conclusion in still other words. As Paul Krugman writes, "International trade is really just a production technique, a way to produce importables indirectly by first producing exportables, then exchanging them."[8] It allows a country to indirectly produce and consume more through exchange than it could otherwise (i.e., by doing everything domestically).

Comparative advantage between two countries is always symmetric: one country has a comparative advantage in one good, the other country in another one. A comparative advantage will exist provided only that the relative internal costs of the two goods are different between the two countries—that is, the rates at which residents can "transform" one good into the other (by moving resources) are different. (In technical parlance, each country will have a comparative advantage if the internal *opportunity costs* of the two goods are different from one country to the other.) In that case, there is a price ratio between the two goods (or *term of trade*) at which trade is beneficial to both countries. A moment of thought will reveal that this intermediate price ratio will lie between the two internal price ratios: each country exports its good for a higher price that its internal cost, and imports the other good for a lower price than its internal cost. Hence, each country reaps an advantage.

Note again that this symmetric or matching comparative advantage occurs even if one country has an absolute advantage over the other. Even if the United States can produce both more machinery and more clothing than Bangladesh, it can obtain still more clothing by specializing in machinery production and trading part of its output for clothes. And even if Bangladesh is less efficient in the production of both machinery and clothes, it can obtain more machinery by producing it indirectly—that is, by exchanging part of its clothes production for imported machinery.

An alternative way to grasp comparative advantage is to understand that a poor country's low productivity (it is poor precisely because productivity is low) is more than compensated for by its low wages; and, on the other side of the trade, a rich country's high wages are more than compensated for by its high productivity. But this offsetting only holds true for the goods in which each country has a comparative advantage; otherwise, the compensation does not happen. For instance, Bangladesh's low wages do not compensate for its low productivity in machinery production, and America's high productivity in clothing does not compensate for its high wages.

The crucial point is that differences within countries in the relative (internal) costs of producing goods and services are what generate comparative advantage and an opportunity for mutually beneficial exchange. Mutually beneficial exchange can coexist with absolute advantage.

Why does comparative advantage lead to beneficial trade? Go back to the example of the accountant and the mechanic: because each has different comparative capabilities, they both benefit from specializing and exchanging, even if the accountant is also more efficient at car repairs. It's the same between two countries. Even if one country is better at everything than the other—for example, the United States in relation to Bangladesh—the former will find it advantageous to specialize in the good for which its advantage is larger; the latter, even if it is less good at everything, will find it advantageous to specialize in the good for which its disadvantage is smaller. By exchanging, each country can finally obtain more than if it had not engaged in trade. Each "produces" through imports what would be most costly to produce at home, in exchange for what it produces at lower cost. Thus, each obtains more for less.

When critics of free trade do address the theory of comparative advantage, they argue that either (1) it relies on a too-simple model or (2) it does not consider that capital is now mobile across countries, contrary to what Ricardo assumed. The first objection is easily disposed of: to understand the world, to avoid seeing it as a confused blob, the analyst needs simplified models of reality. Of course, we must verify that the predictions of the simple model conform to what we observe in the real world, but there is no other way to understand than by going from the simple to the complicated. As for the second objection, factor mobility does not change the essential conclusions of the theory of comparative advantage. A country will always have some comparative advantage, if only because of its geographical location and other characteristics such as its history, institutions, and culture. Ultimately, comparative advantage will play out among individuals and companies trading across borders the same way it works within a country.[9] In fact, this is what we observe in international supply chains (see essay 1 at the end of this chapter).

Another objection is that empirical evidence does not confirm the theoretical conclusion of total specialization. The United States, for example, does not totally specialize in machinery, but keeps producing a small volume of clothes. This problem with the theory can be overcome by dropping the simplifying assumption that production costs are constant. If one assumes instead that the more machinery is produced, the higher the cost will be in terms of forgone clothing (because, say, the machinery industry will have to employ less-skilled seamstresses to work in machinery-making factories), the United States may stop specializing before no clothes at all are manufactured here. Note also that complex goods like an automobile or a smartphone can contain parts manufactured in different countries on the basis of finer-grain comparative advantages along complex supply chains. Moreover, goods and services are heterogeneous (for example, there are many sorts of textiles, even in a given fiber), so there is scope for intra-industry specialization and trade.[10] It is thus easy to understand that the United States both imports and exports cars, for example, and that some of these cars may contain parts manufactured in Canada, Mexico, or other parts of the world. For a large country like the United States, geographical distance also plays a role: some goods cost less to import from an adjacent country than to purchase from a domestic producer on the other side of the home country.

Another issue not addressed by the theory of comparative advantage is the changes in the distribution of income that trade brings within a trading country. Although trade increases total income (the sum of all individual incomes), some groups may lose—such as labor that is displaced by foreign competition. (This issue is addressed in chapter 6, as well as in essay 6.)

Despite all these qualifications, empirical evidence seems to confirm that "productivity differences play an important role in international trade and that it is comparative rather than absolute advantage that matters."[11] The classic demonstration was given by Béla Balassa just after World War II. Balassa showed that, although the US economy had an absolute advantage over the British economy (all manufacturing industries were more productive in the United States than in the United Kingdom), the ratio of US exports to British exports diminished as the US comparative advantage became lower. The United Kingdom exported relatively more of what it had a comparative advantage in, and the United States exported relatively less of what it did not have a comparative advantage in.[12] The recent rise of poor countries in some specialized markets (clothing, textiles, furniture, call centers, and others) shows the explanatory power of the theory of comparative advantage.

Economic analysis shows not only that a country is able to compete against low-cost producers, but also that it has (that is, its producers have) an interest in doing so, as long as it specializes in goods in which it has a comparative advantage. In these areas of comparative advantage, the higher productivity of labor more than offsets its higher remuneration. Labor is generally more productive in rich countries (this is why they are rich) because it has more physical capital (machines and equipment) to work with, and because the workers have more human capital (knowledge and skills). Rich countries also have better physical infrastructure, more trust, and better legal institutions, all of which are kinds of capital and contribute to increasing the productivity of workers.[13]

For examples of higher productivity compensating for lower foreign wages, consider that the average manufacturing wage in Mexico is $4.50 an hour, compared to $19.50 in the United States.[14] This does not prevent American producers from exporting (among other things) corn, soybeans, and plastics to Mexico—obviously because the productivity of American workers in these sectors (or subsectors of them) is high enough to compensate for their much higher wages. On the other side of the trade, Mexican workers' low wages compensate for their lower productivity in some sectors, so that that they succeed in exporting their products (such as optical and medical instruments, furniture and bedding, and fresh vegetables) to American buyers.[15] Similarly, Vietnamese producers are able to export clothes to American consumers because wages in Vietnam are lower than the low labor productivity in that country. But American producers can still export machinery and transportation equipment to Vietnam because the productivity of American labor in this sector is higher than wages on the American market.

Comparative advantages, not absolute advantages or the general level of wages, drive international trade. Because of this, American producers are able to compete with low-wage countries in goods and services for which the comparative advantage lies with America.

ESSAY 1: COMPARATIVE ADVANTAGE
AND SUPPLY CHAINS

Comparative advantage is the benefit that a trading country accrues when it can produce a good or service at a lower relative cost to itself (in terms of other goods) than another country can, so that it can export the good or service to the other country at a mutually beneficial price. Even if one country has an *absolute* disadvantage in terms of productivity, other countries will generally find it advantageous to purchase what the unproductive country has a comparative advantage in producing.

Each country benefits—that is, its producers benefit— from specializing in the goods and services in which the country has a comparative advantage: these are what it can sell to foreign countries. Bangladesh producers benefit from producing apparel and footwear, and American consumers benefit from importing these goods from Bangladesh. American producers benefit from producing airliners, and airlines operating in Bangladesh (and their customers) benefit from purchasing them. American producers benefit from producing software and from conceiving and designing electronic devices, and consumers all around the world benefit from importing these goods and devices. Producers in many poor countries benefit from specializing in assembling devices conceived and designed elsewhere.

Econometric research generally confirms that trade increases per capita income. The International Monetary Fund, the World Bank, and the World Trade Organization report that "a one-percentage-point increase in trade openness raises real per capita income by 2 to 6 percent."[16] International trade (often measured, like trade openness, by adding imports and exports) has increased from 24 percent of world GDP in 1960 to 58 percent in 2015, which implies a very large impact on per capita income. According to one conservative estimate, if the trade liberalization since World War II had not occurred, American GDP would have been lower by 7.3 percent in 2003.[17] A more recent estimate suggests that, without trade liberalization, American GDP per capita would have been 12 percent lower in 2016, but this estimate incorporates the impact of lower transportation and telecommunications costs and technology spillovers besides trade liberalization proper.[18] Without trade liberalization, however, the impact of these other factors would presumably have been much dampened. One way or another, trade accounts for an important proportion of American and world GDP.

Supply Chains

One aspect of comparative advantage is that different firms within an industry—say, within automobile or aircraft manufacturing—specialize in different parts of the final product or inputs into the production process. With specialization and globalization, supply chains have become more complex and often extend over multiple countries. Boeing imports large components of its 787 Dreamliner from manufacturers all over the world: the mid-forward fuselage and the wings from Japan, the Rolls-Royce engines from the United Kingdom, the center fuselage from Italy, the passenger entry doors from France, the cargo access doors from Sweden, the wing tips from Korea, the rudder from China, and so on.[19] The dense supply chains between the United

States and Mexico offer another example of integration: an unfinished product often crosses the border many times.

US Comparative Advantage

Although American manufacturing remains vibrant in certain areas (see chapter 4 and essay 4), the country's comparative advantage has shifted toward services, as has been the case in many other advanced economies. Figure 1.1 shows how exports of American services have grown much more rapidly than exports of manufactured goods and agricultural products. Services now represent one-third of all American exports.[20]

The whole service sector now employs more than 80 percent of American workers. It includes health, education, and housing, which mostly comprise non-traded items.

Figure 1.1. US Exports by Sector, 1980–2014

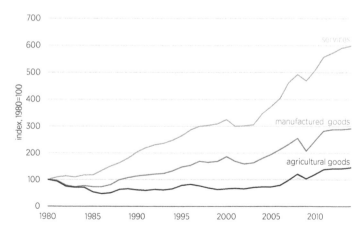

Note: Data are corrected for inflation.
Source: Council of Economic Advisers, *The Economic Benefits of U.S. Trade*, May 2015.

But many foreigners do come to the United States to pur-chase education and health services, which are exports from the point of view of Americans. Anything sold to a foreign resident by an American resident is an export, whether the foreigner buys it in the United States or has the good deliv-ered to his country. In all these cases, American resources (labor, capital, land) are used to produce something sold to a foreign tourist (personal, business, or medical), a foreign student, or a foreign importer. The main services exported from America are travel (for example, when foreign residents travel on US airlines or foreign tourists buy goods and ser-vices in the United States), intellectual property (for example, charges for licenses of US technology), transport (the cost of shipping goods to foreigners on American ships, planes, or trucks), finance and insurance, and other business services such as advertising, telecommunications, computer and data processing, and accounting and legal services.[21] The United States has a large trade surplus in the service sector.

The United States also has a comparative advantage in many agricultural products, such as oilseeds and grains; agri-culture shows a trade surplus. Trade results also suggest that the United States has a comparative advantage in many spe-cialized manufacturing subsectors, such as aircraft, machin-ery, and oil products. The textile manufacturers that continue operating in the United States have specialized in what they have a comparative advantage in, and are often thriving in export markets. For example, Milliken & Company of Spar-tanburg, South Carolina, has developed bandages for burn victims, a fabric that snuffs out fires, and a cloth that turns into concrete when it is hosed down.[22]

CHAPTER 2

Objection: Free Trade Harms the United States

Protectionists frequently claim that free trade harms the United States. This is a fuzzy argument as long as it doesn't specify what is the alleged harm and who exactly is the victim. Later chapters will consider objections related to specific harms: the trade deficit (chapter 3), loss of manufacturing (chapter 4), loss of jobs (chapter 5), and lowering of wages (chapter 6). One way to construe a general argument for the harmful character of free international trade is to posit that its costs outweigh its benefits. In other words, perhaps trade harms the United States because its costs, in terms of imports, are higher than its benefits, measured by exports. Indeed, US imports have been larger than exports since the 1970s.

The main problem with this argument is that it inverses the costs and benefits of trade. In reality, imports are the benefits that flow from trade; exports are the costs. Moreover, when we use a methodologically correct method to calculate costs and benefits, it can be shown that the benefits of free trade are actually larger than its costs. This chapter demonstrates these two points.

Imports Are a Benefit; Exports Are a Cost

The mercantilists of the 16th to 18th centuries thought that a country should export as much as possible and import as little as possible. This is an economic error. Just as individuals sell goods or labor *in order to* buy something, countries export in order to import. As James Mill wrote nearly 200 years ago, "The benefit which is derived from exchanging one commodity for another, arises, in all cases, from the commodity *received*, not from the commodity given."[1] Exports are a cost because the United States uses its resources to produce goods and services for foreign countries; imports are a benefit because the United States uses the resources of foreign countries to obtain its own goods and services. So, contrary to what the mercantilists thought, the United States should import as much as it can and export as little as possible (assuming it were possible to maintain this regime for long). A *reductio ad absurdum* of the mercantilist argument is easy. Imagine that the United States ships its exports by sea and that the returning ships bring back imported goods. If the returning ships sank, would this situation of exports without imports be a benefit for the United States?[2] Obviously not.

The term "concessions" used in international trade negotiations to describe the imports that a country will accept in exchange for the exports it wants to ship is deeply misleading. This is an important point to grasp in order to understand the economic approach to trade. For the country's residents, the so-called concessions are the benefits, while exports are the costs. Jagdish Bhagdwati, a leading contemporary trade economist, expresses the same idea:

> There is a danger that excessive use of the language of "concessions" in trade bargaining can lead, and has indeed led, to a widespread bureaucratic and political acceptance of the wrong-headed view that import liberalization is expensive

rather than gainful and must be offset by concessions for one's exports.[3]

The argument that the United States uses its resources to produce goods and services for exportation needs to be qualified. In a free country, resources belong not to the country as a single entity ("us") but to different individuals or private groups (including corporations) separately. America is not a single entity but the collection of millions of individual Americans. At least in a free society, "country" is just shorthand for the individuals who compose it.[4] It follows that free trade can harm a country only if it harms the individuals who constitute the country.

In economics, exchange and its benefits occupy a central place. The basic idea is that both parties derive benefits (or at least expect to benefit) from any exchange in which they voluntarily participate; otherwise, at least one party would have declined the deal. The benefits of exchange obviously apply to trade between a national and a foreigner, which is nothing but an exchange over a political border. How could free trade harm the country if it benefits the individuals who compose it?

Free Trade Carries Net Benefits

Of course, some individuals may lose—for example, the shareholders of the corporations outcompeted by foreign firms or the workers who have to find a new job in another company or industry. It can be shown, however, that individuals generally benefit from free international trade. We have already presented one demonstration: if the producers of a country specialize in what they have a comparative advantage in, and if consumers are free to import what can be produced more efficiently abroad, then each country ends up with more goods and services. Economic theory provides another sort of demonstration by following what happens when a protective measure such as a tariff or an equivalent quota is applied or repealed. Using this approach, it can be proved that, in virtually all cases, protection generates a net cost compared to free trade or, alternatively, free trade generates a net benefit compared to protection.[5]

A tariff increases the domestic price of a good, including the price in the market share supplied by domestic producers; indeed, that is precisely why the tariff is imposed. In the general case of an unchanged world price, a tariff will end up being paid entirely by domestic consumers in the form of a higher price. (The world price of a good is the price at which it can be imported in world markets.) The tariff is added to the unchanged world price for the consumers of the country in which it is imposed. Domestic consumers lose and domestic producers gain, but the consumers lose more than the producers gain, so the tariff creates a net loss. Why is this true? Because if a tariff had net benefits, it would not be necessary: domestic producers could, by lowering prices in the normal course of competition, attract consumers into patronizing them instead of buying imports. The fact that domestic producers cannot do this proves that they gain less from protection than consumers lose; or, seen from the other side, that the loss suffered by producers from free trade is more than offset by the gains to consumers.

When the protectionist measure used is a tariff—as opposed to an import quota or a subsidy to domestic producers—the proof is not complete, and requires a second step. The previously determined net cost of the tariff must be reduced by the tariff revenues that flow to the federal treasury's coffers. In addition to paying an excess price to domestic producers, consumers pay foreign producers an excess price that is equivalent to the tariff the latter have to pay. So part of what the tariff forces consumers to pay will be returned to them in their capacity as recipients of government services (assuming the government does not waste the money).

Of course, this does not mean that each consumer will receive in augmented government services exactly what he or she has paid in tariffs on the protected good. Typically, some will receive more and others less, depending how much of the tariffed good they buy and how much of the government services they consume. Some government redistribution is involved, even if it is impossible to quantify with any precision. It is not only trade liberalization that causes complex redistribution effects; protectionism does, too.

One might think a tariff would have no net cost because what consumers lose is gained by domestic producers *and* by the domestic treasury. But this is not true. What domestic producers and the treasury receive does not totally offset the cost to consumers of the protected good. There remains a net cost that economists call a *deadweight loss*. Deadweight loss measures the distortion in the allocation of resources. Domestic resources that were previously used, and could still be used, to produce other goods are reallocated to produce domestically an additional quantity of the protected good. This is because the higher price domestic producers can get incites them to spend more and increase the quantity they supply. This increased domestic output is a waste and produces a deadweight loss because the good in question could be (and was before) imported at a better price, while domestic producers were able to produce something else instead. Another component of the deadweight loss is what consumers lose because they decrease the quantity they demand—their total consumption—of the protected good because its price has increased on the domestic market. The deadweight loss is a straight waste that benefits no one: domestic resources are used to produce something that could be imported more cheaply, and consumers have to reduce their consumption. Since something is wasted, the total cost of the tariff for consumers is higher than its total benefits for domestic producers. Conversely, free trade carries net benefits in the sense that all individuals could potentially benefit by the removal of the deadweight loss or waste.

According to most economists, the only serious challenge to the demonstration just presented is the *optimal tariff* argument. This argument posits a special case in which the world price of a good is not fixed, as was assumed previously. Suppose country H is so large compared to the world market for good f that its demand for imports affects the world price of the good. If country H imposes a tariff on good f, thereby diminishing its own demand for f, the price of good f will decline in international markets. This is because country H is, by assumption, important enough to influence the price on the world market for f. In other words, country H's terms of trade, defined as the ratio of the price of its exports to the price of imports, have increased—that is, they have become more favorable.[6] Country H can now get more imports for a given quantity of exports. If this effect is large enough, it can potentially more than cancel the deadweight loss caused by the tariff, bringing a net gain for the protectionist country. This is why such a tariff is called an *optimal* tariff.

The optimal tariff argument applies only to large countries whose trade can affect world prices. An optimal tariff cannot help small or poor countries, for the optimal tariff there is zero. What does this imply for the United States? The United States is certainly a large country in terms of the size of its economy. American imports make up about 17 percent of the total world merchandise imports, compared with 14 percent for the European Union (counted as a bloc) and 13 percent for China.[7] And the United States accounts for a fourth of world GDP.[8] However, the optimal tariff argument applies only to specific markets in which the large country can move prices. With regard to the American economy, it may apply to, say, large airliners, but arguably not to most imported goods. Furthermore, there is no optimal tariff if retaliation by other countries leads to a trade war, in which many countries raise protectionist barriers and all lose because of reduced trade. In general, it is fair to say that the truly optimal tariff is zero.

Note that, unlike an optimal tariff, an export subsidy can never be optimal—that is, it can never carry net benefits for the residents of the country whose government does the subsidization. Suppose H is a large country whose government subsidizes the export of widgets. The supply of widgets will increase and their price will fall on world markets. Consumers of widgets in both H and foreign countries benefit, as do the producers subsidized in H. But the terms of trade of H have *deteriorated*, as it now gets a lower price for is imports, so there is no improvement in the terms of trade that could compensate for the deadweight loss that subsidies (like taxes or tariffs) cause. Moreover, with subsidies to exports instead of tariffs on imports, money flows out, not into, the treasury. So treasury revenues cannot compensate for the deadweight loss either. Even in a small country, export subsidies will carry a net cost because they represent a straight transfer from domestic taxpayers to domestic producers, and the existence of a deadweight loss implies that the latter gain less than the former lose.

We can now understand how the Chinese government's subsidization of products like steel or solar panels hurts the Chinese even more than does a straight domestic subsidy with no impact on world prices. Because China is a large producer of steel and solar panels on world markets, the subsidies push down the world prices of the subsidized products, which means that China's terms of trade deteriorate. Foreign consumers, including American consumers, benefit from the lower world prices, but Chinese residents (except for the producers) bear the cost. How long will the hapless Chinese accept this?

Another reason to doubt the benefit of an optimal tariff for a large country is the integration of supply chains. Because the world economy has become more integrated and efficient, many supply chains extend over several countries, and a significant portion of a country's production and exports incorporates imported inputs that are rendered more expensive by tariffs and other trade barriers. It is estimated that over one-half of all US imports serve as intermediate inputs in domestic production processes.[9] Conversely, many goods imported into the United States have American contents. A smartphone imported from China has typically been designed and engineered in California and was only assembled in China, with components made or designed in half a dozen Asian and European countries and metals from Africa. "Likewise," notes the *Economist*, "every dollar of Mexican exports contains around 40 cents of American output embedded within it."[10]

We must remember that the usual way of speaking about "countries" importing or exporting is merely a linguistic shortcut. Individuals and firms are the ones that import or export, not countries. Countries or societies are collections of individuals, not superorganisms. All benefits accrue to individuals and all costs are paid by individuals. This approach is based on methodological individualism, the theory that we understand society and the economy by explaining individual actions and their consequences.[11] In a free country, the idea that individuals are the actors is also recognized as a political value. Saying that the benefits of free trade for a country are greater than its costs means that individuals in this country obtain, in total, more benefits than costs.

For all these reasons, we may confidently conclude that free trade brings net benefits to a country and that, on the contrary, it is protectionism that harms a country. Or, expressing this conclusion more correctly, free trade brings benefits to most residents of a country, while protectionism harms them.

ESSAY 2: IMPORTS ARE *NOT* A DEDUCTION FROM GDP

One common argument, often echoed by financial journalists, is that imports are "a subtraction in the calculation of GDP." In a letter to the *Wall Street Journal*, future Commerce secretary Wilbur Ross repeated the error. "It's Econ 101 that GDP equals the sum of domestic economic activity plus 'net exports,' i.e., exports minus imports," he wrote. "Therefore, when we run massive and chronic trade deficits, it weakens our economy."[12] The implication is that if imports and the trade deficit are reduced, GDP will expand.

This is not Econ 101 at all. It is the opposite of what any macroeconomics textbook explains.[13] And the argument is false according to simple accounting. It comes from a misunderstanding of an accounting identity used in the national income and product accounts:

$$GDP = C + I + G + X - M,$$

which says that GDP is spent on consumer expenditures (C), business investment (I), government expenditures (G), and the difference between exports (X) and imports (M).

The equation can be written as

$$GDP = C + I + G + (X - M),$$

which seems to imply that a trade surplus, a positive $(X - M)$, adds to GDP, whereas a trade deficit, a negative $(X - M)$, subtracts from it. At any rate, somebody not familiar with national accounting will, like Ross, deduce that imports reduce GDP. This deduction is wrong.

What happens is that C, I, and G already include imported goods and services. The Chinese-made fishing rod a customer bought at Walmart was captured in C; the printing press a newspaper company bought from Germany was part of I; and the salary of the foreign consultant hired by the government was included in G. M is subtracted on the right side of the equation to exclude those imports from the calculation of GDP.

As its name indicates, gross *domestic* product is the sum of all goods and services produced within a country's territory. So the term −M is used to cancel the imports that are hidden in C, I, and G. Imports are not deducted from GDP. They cannot reduce the statistical measure of GDP because, by definition, they are not part of it.[14]

American consumers and businesses do use part of the GDP they produce—that is, their incomes—to import goods and services, but this does not mean that it reduces their production. If you buy a home appliance imported from China, you are not reducing your salary by doing so, but using what you have earned to obtain something that is worth more to you than the dollars you earned.

CHAPTER 3

Objection: The Trade Deficit Is Bad

Wilbur Ross, who later became Commerce secretary, wrote that imports reduce GDP in national accounting—which is an elementary error, as we saw in essay 2. But even if Ross's statement is a straight *accounting* error, we should pay attention to the *economic* argument that the trade deficit is bad. Maybe there are ways in which the trade deficit reduces GDP. Perhaps imported goods and services prevent the production of equivalents at home? One may also think that when we import more than we export, we have to borrow to make up the difference, thereby indebting the country vis-à-vis the rest of the world.

The trade-deficit objection is a restatement of the old mercantilist argument that a country should export as much as possible and import as little as possible. The balance of trade, technically called the goods and services balance, is the difference between total exports and total imports of goods and services; it is deemed "negative," "unfavorable," or "in deficit" when imports exceed exports, and "positive," "favorable," or "in surplus" in the opposite case. The trade-deficit or balance-of-trade objection ignores the fact that imports are important because they directly satisfy consumers' preferences; exports are only an indirect means to that end, in the same way that an individual sells in order to purchase. However, the trade-deficit objection is worth treating separately.

What's Wrong with Trade or Current-Account Deficits?

There is nothing inherently good or inherently bad about a trade deficit. For some countries to have surpluses, others must have deficits. A country's trade deficit or surplus is simply the sum of the surpluses and deficits of all the individuals in that country in relation to foreigners. If two groups of individuals were chosen at random within a given territory, it is likely that one would have a trade deficit with the other, and the other a trade surplus. So there seems no reason to be concerned about territorial or national trade deficits. For example, the US trade balance has been negative since the 1970s without any noticeable problem, whereas it was positive during the two world wars and the Great Depression.[1] (Note that the trade deficit and all other measures of the international balance of payments are flows over a certain period of time—a quarter or a year—not stocks.)

Within the US trade balance, or balance of goods and services, the balance of goods is negative (−$753 billion in 2016) and the balance of services is positive (+$248 billion), resulting in a trade deficit of $505 billion. The *trade balance* is only part—albeit the largest part—of America's *current account*. The other major component of the current account is payments received by US residents on assets held abroad, which can be thought of as exports of capital services, and payments sent abroad on foreign assets held in the United States, which can be viewed as imports of capital services. The balance on those other items is positive. Including all components of the current account, the US deficit is reduced to $452 billion.[2]

The Other Side of the Balance of International Payments

The second side of a country's balance of payment, the financial account, shows the flow of money and other financial instruments that corresponds to the flow of goods and services on the current account. It includes net borrowing or lending abroad, net foreign portfolio investment, net foreign direct investment, and a few other items. As a matter of accounting (debits equal credits), the balance of the financial account must exactly compensate, with an opposite sign, the current-account balance. A deficit on the current account is thus the mirror image of a financial surplus.

What is of interest is not the accounting identity (which is true by definition) but the real-world adjustments that equalize the two sides of a country's balance of payments. The foreign exchange rate—the price of dollars in foreign currencies—is one such adjustment mechanism. If American consumers wanted to continuously import more than American producers export, and if foreign investors did not want to invest in America enough to compensate, the dollar would fall, reducing imports and increasing foreign investment.

It is tempting to interpret the financial account as the means by which a current-account balance is financed (foreigners lend to Americans in order to allow Americans to import more) or, alternatively, as a way to dispose of a surplus of foreign currency (Chinese investors use it to invest overseas). This interpretation is at best misleading because the two sides of the balance of international payments describe actions that are largely independent. Consumers do not import only because the US dollar is high, but basically because of comparative advantage. Foreign investors do not bring capital into the United States only because they do not know what to do with their dollars, but also because America offers good investment opportunities. In the US Net International Investment Position (the stock result of the annual flows of the balance of payments), more than 40 percent of "U.S. liabilities" are direct investments and equity portfolio investments, which are not "debt" in any conventional sense.[3]

The relationship between the current account and the financial account goes both ways. The attractiveness of America for foreign capital also influences imports. Other things being equal, any foreign inflow of capital contributes to a current-account deficit: the flow of euros for investment in America pushes the euro down and the dollar up, encouraging American consumers to import more. The American current-account deficit is in large part a reflection of the fact that foreigners want to invest in America. From this perspective, the current-account deficit is not a cause of American decline but, on the contrary, a consequence of America's growth and attractiveness to investors. Moreover, the financial account surplus reflects a situation where American residents' savings are less than new investment opportunities in America. The gap between savings by American residents and new investment opportunities is covered by foreign loans and investment in American businesses.[4] This explanation of current-account deficits is widely accepted by economists: the *Economist* explains, "America's overall balance of trade is ultimately determined by its investment and saving."[5]

Some people express the fear that a surplus on the financial account—which means more investment and lending in America from foreigners than there is investment and lending overseas by American residents—implies that "our" debt toward foreigners increases and that our children will have to repay it. In some sense, this is true: when foreigners invest in America or lend to American firms, they thereby obtain a claim to future production in American territory. They will use their future profits in dollars to buy American goods; or, what amounts to the same thing, they will sell the dollars to others, push down the rate of exchange, and increase American exports or reduce the imports available to Americans. The reality, however, is a bit more complicated.

To the extent that these foreign profits on investment in the United States are claims on future private production, they are not claims against what Americans currently own, but rather claims on new production made possible by the investment that the foreigners themselves contribute. Moreover, American workers are made more productive by the supplementary capital invested in the firms they work for, and these workers will earn more than they would have earned without the foreign investment. It's a win-win situation: as in any free exchange, no contracting party loses.

The fear that foreign investment will translate into claims against all Americans, however, becomes justified when the money is lent to the government for unproductive or wasteful activities, such as various forms of redistribution. The use of foreign savings by the federal government is far from insignificant. The (federal) debt held by the public (which includes the foreign "public") currently increases by about $1 trillion per year. It is estimated that 45 percent of that public debt is held by foreign investors and foreign governments, including foreign central banks.[6] Assuming that foreigners continue to purchase American public debt instruments in the same proportion, foreigners lend the federal government some $450 billion per year, which enters as an inflow in the financial account of the US balance of payments. This amount accounts for virtually all the US current-account deficit (which, as previously stated, was $452 billion in 2016). It is as if, every year, the federal government gave some $450 billion in claims to foreigners against the future production of American taxpayers. At any rate, these numbers suggest that the federal government's contribution to the current-account deficit is large. When the government borrows from foreigners, the result is an upward pressure on the current-account deficit.

But all this should be taken as an argument against federal deficits and the continuous increase of the public debt, not against current-account deficits or trade deficits per se.

Trade or current-account deficits, then, are not inherently problematic. They reflect the relationship between a country's economy and the outside world—in the case of the United States, a relationship that is marked by the country's attractiveness to foreign investors and the wealth of domestic consumers.[7] Another reason not to worry about consolidated national trade surpluses and deficits is that, in a free economy, each individual and corporation takes care of its own surplus or deficit. And, back to first principles, one must remember that imports are what matter. Condemning a trade deficit per se is condemning imports, which are the benefits from trade, in favor of exports, which represent the cost of trade.

The Case for Unilateral Free Trade

The case against trade or current-account deficits is so weak that one can argue in favor of declaring unilateral free trade—that is, completely liberalizing imports and letting the balance of payments take care of itself. In a very real sense, free trade does not require free trade agreements but can be declared unilaterally, which is what the British government more or less did in the middle of the 19th century. Paul Krugman writes,

> If economists ruled the world, there would be no need for a World Trade Organization. The economist's case for free trade is essentially a unilateral case: a country serves its own interests by pursuing free trade regardless of what other countries may do.[8]

One way to understand this is to realize that a country must export if it is to import. Otherwise, where would it get the foreign currency it needs to import? On the other side of the trade, a protectionist country cannot just export without importing (or investing in foreign countries)—otherwise what would it do with its foreign exchange earnings? Hence, unilateral free trade promotes exports as much as imports, at least over time. Leaving a country's residents free to import guarantees that matching exports will be forthcoming. As defined in the introduction of this book, free trade is unhindered exchanges between individuals over political borders, and its real, practical content is the liberty to import unimpeded by one's own government.

If a foreign government is protectionist, the second-best option is for the US government to maintain freedom to import for its own residents. As economist Joan Robinson remarked, protectionist retaliation looks as sensible as "dump[ing] rocks into our harbors because other nations have rocky coasts."[9] National welfare is not increased by responding to protectionism with protectionism (unless the bluff works and serves to liberalize trade instead of starting a trade war). In most cases, retaliatory protectionism is like saying to the foreign protectionist government, "You hurt your subjects? I will hurt mine, too. Take that!"[10]

The freedom to export in the sense of the absence of export restraints *imposed by one's own government* is also important. I have not emphasized this point because, in the current mercantilist context, governments threaten mainly the freedom to import. But the prohibition of oil exports (with a few exceptions) by the American government until the end of 2015[11] should remind us that the freedom to export can also be threatened by one's own government in the name of protectionism.[12]

There is little reason to believe that freer trade will lead to an undesirable trade or current-account deficit. Importing goods and services does not merely prevent the production of the equivalents at home; it prevents the production of more costly domestic substitutes. Protectionism replaces imports with domestic production that, if reallocated, could buy more imported goods than are produced at home. Moreover, the demand for foreign goods—say, foreign luxury cars—can motivate Americans to produce more in order to earn more and satisfy that demand. Remember that consumption is the goal, and production just a means. Finally, a trade deficit does not push Americans into debt or impoverish them. Unless it is fueled by government deficits, it allows foreign investors to create factories, industrial equipment, warehouses, commercial buildings, and other capital goods that can only benefit most Americans, workers and consumers alike.

ESSAY 3: THE BALANCE OF TRADE

The *balance of trade* (or *trade balance*), technically called the *goods and services balance*, is the difference between the total exports and total imports of goods and services by a country's residents. Many people focus on the trade balance because it is the most important component of the overall current-account balance in the balance of international payments, and because it receives the most attention in public debates.

Table 3.1 provides the main numbers for the US balance of payments in 2016. It consists of two accounts: the current account (rows 1–11) and the financial account (of which only the balance is shown here, on row 12).

Consider first the current account, which shows a negative balance of $452 billion (row 11). Within the current account, the trade balance (balance on goods and services) shows a deficit of $505 billion (row 9). We may want to focus on the balance of goods only or on the *merchandise balance*, with a deficit of $753 billion (row 3). (*Merchandise* means the same as *goods*.) The balance of services is positive, so it is the trade in goods that generates the negative trade balance. Another reason for sometimes focusing on merchandise trade is that historical statistics before 1929 include only goods, not services.

Second, consider the *financial account*, which shows the net inflows and outflows of foreign investment and lending to the United States, the balance of which must be the mirror image of the current-account balance, as shown by rows 11 and 12. The net financial inflow is a positive $452 billion. The simplest way to grasp the identity between the current and

Table 3.1. US International Transactions (Balance of Payments), 2016

Current account (in billions of dollars)

1	Exports of goods		1,456
2	Imports of goods*		−2,208
3	Balance on goods (or merchandise)	row 1+row 2:	−753
4	Exports of services		752
5	Imports of services*		−505
6	Balance on services	row 4+row 5:	247
7	Exports of goods and services*	row 1+row 4:	2,208
8	Imports of goods and services	row 2+row 5:	−2,713
9	Balance on goods and services (trade balance)*	row 7+row 8 (or row 3+row 6):	−505
10	Balance on other current-account items		53
11	Balance on current account**		−452

Financial account (in billions of dollars)

12	Balance on financial account***		452

*The equality of lines 2 and 7 and the equality of lines 5 and 9 are statistical flukes due to rounding.
**Including "capital account."
***Including statistical discrepancy.
Source: Bureau of Economic Analysis, table 1.1, "U.S. International Transactions," June 20, 2017. Totals may not add up exactly because of rounding.

financial accounts is to reflect that the number of US dollars entering the country must be equal to the number leaving. Otherwise, the exchange rate will move to equalize the two sides of the balance of payments.

The historical perspective is given by figure 3.1, which shows the imports and exports of merchandise from 1790 to 2016. The values are expressed as proportions of GDP in order to make them more comparable over time. The distance between the two curves measures the balance of goods in proportion of GDP. (Note that data before 1929 are much less reliable than data for the subsequent years.)

The chart clearly shows the merchandise trade deficit that appeared in the mid-1970s and grew rapidly. This deficit is of no significance per se. We export in order to import, not the other way around, and the more imports we obtain for our exports, the better. The idea of having favorable "terms of trade" for a country means precisely that: getting more

Figure 3.1. US Imports and Exports of Merchandise as a Proportion of GDP, 1790–2016

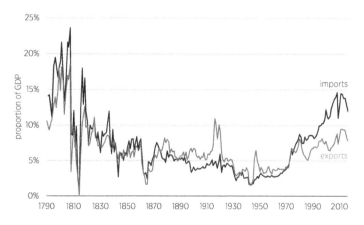

Sources: For 1929 and later: Bureau of Economic Analysis, table 1.1.5, "Gross Domestic Product," June 28, 2017, lines 1, 17, and 20. For merchandise exports and imports before 1929: US Census Bureau, *Bicentennial Edition: Historical Statistics of the United States, Colonial Times to 1970*, series U 190 and U 193. Estimates for GDP before 1929 are from Louis Johnston and Samuel H. Williamson, "What Was the U.S. GDP Then?," *Measuring Worth*, 2017.

for less. However, the trade deficit becomes a problem to the extent that it is generated by the budget deficit of the federal government: because domestic savings are too low for what private borrowers and the federal government want to borrow, foreign savings are attracted, push the dollar up, and generate a trade deficit.

Figure 3.1 suggests that the balance of merchandise trade was mostly "negative" between the time of the founding and the last third of the 19th century. Economist Robert E. Lipsey writes that "for most of the period from the inauguration of George Washington to the end of the 19th century, the United States imported more merchandise than it exported," and that "the United States was a net borrower from countries throughout the 19th century."[13] This is not surprising. As a developing country, America required a high level of foreign investment, which leads to a high deficit on the current account. The balance of trade then turned positive for most of the 100 years running from the mid-1870s to the mid-1970s.

Merchandise trade surpluses and deficits have generally been a small proportion of GDP. They have been higher lately, at 4 percent to 6 percent of GDP, for two reasons: the attractiveness of the American economy to foreign investors and the large budget deficits at the federal level. In fact, the annual purchase of federal debt by foreigners probably accounts for most of the current account deficit.

In an accounting sense, the balance of payments is always in equilibrium. The exchange rate adjusts given the demand of importers, exporters, American investors abroad, and foreign investors in America. Except for the federal borrowing needs, there would be no reason to be concerned about a deficit on the current-account side of the balance of payments.

Not surprisingly, there appears to be no relationship between the trade deficit and the unemployment rate, as shown in figure 3.2. There is no statistically significant correlation between the trade deficit as a proportion of GDP and unemployment rates over the period 1960–2016 (the longest series available for the trade deficit). It is only in the 1960s that we observe trade surpluses (the positive range of the horizontal axis) and low unemployment rates. Since then, trade deficits have prevailed, but have been accompanied by varying rates of unemployment. Since the Great Recession,

Figure 3.2. Unemployment Rate and Trade Deficit or Surplus, 1960–2016

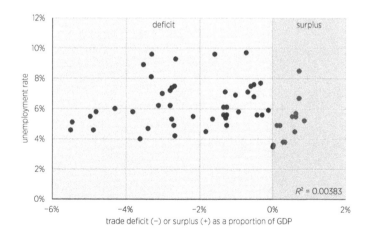

Sources: Bureau of Labor Statistics, "Unemployment Rate 16 Years and Older," series LNU0400; Bureau of Economic Analysis, table 1.1, "U.S. International Transactions," June 20, 2017; and Bureau of Economic Analysis, table 1.1.5, "Gross Domestic Product," last revised July 28, 2017. All data were extracted on August 5, 2017.

the trade deficit has remained constant (again as a proportion to GDP) while the unemployment rate has continuously diminished.[14] The unemployment rate depends on other factors than the trade balance, including economic growth and the economic cycle.

CHAPTER 4

Objection: The United States Is Losing Its Factories

Since 1999, US imports of manufactured goods have doubled,[1] and manufacturing employment has dropped by 28 percent.[2] Between 2002 and 2012, the number of manufacturing establishments with paid employees decreased by 15 percent.[3] The conclusion seems to follow that the United States is losing its factories because of trade.

These data are real and cause real concern, but they must be interpreted correctly. Before getting into the analysis, it is useful to remember one feature of a free society: "American" factories are in fact owned by multiple private businesses, themselves owned by Americans or foreigners or both. It is true that factories located on US soil employ mainly American residents, but those factories do not belong to their employees—except partially for those who directly or indirectly, through pension funds, for example, own stock in the companies that own the factories.

Manufacturing Has Changed

Manufacturing has changed, and not only in the United States. In the 10 developed countries for which a consistent comparative data series is available from the early 1970s to 2012 (Australia, Canada, France, Germany, Italy, Japan, the Netherlands, Sweden, the United Kingdom, and the United States), the proportion of employment in manufacturing has been declining since the early 1970s, if not before.[4] One study finds that between 1970 and 2007, the unweighted average of the employment share of manufacturing in 19 countries (the United States, Japan, and several Western European countries) dropped by more than 15 percentage points.[5]

In the United States, for which a longer series is available, the proportion of civilian employment in manufacturing reached a peak of 26 percent in 1953 and has since been decreasing nearly nonstop, to 8 percent in 2016.[6] The actual number of manufacturing employees has been on a downward trend since 1979; from a peak of 19,553 million jobs in that year, more than seven million jobs have disappeared.[7] Manufacturing's share (value added) of GDP has dropped from around 25 percent between the end of the 1940s and the end of the 1960s to 12 percent in 2015.[8]

Despite this decline, real manufacturing production has increased by 180 percent from 1972 to 2007, and has nearly recovered the reduction suffered during the 2008–2009 recession.[9] With fewer workers, value added in manufacturing—that is, its contribution to GDP—is up 40 percent since 1997.[10] (See essay 4 for more information.) Manufacturing output has not dropped like employment because labor productivity has increased as a result of a number of factors, including technological progress and long (often multicountry) supply chains. American manufacturing has "declined" mainly in the sense that it has become more productive.

Manufacturing has fundamentally changed globally, and the transformation is not yet complete. The final assembly of components is now the low end of manufacturing. The high-end process consists of conception, research and development, complex manufacturing of components with new techniques such as additive manufacturing (also called 3-D printing), and integrated aftersales service. In developed countries, factories are now places in which highly trained engineers, designers, and technicians work with a small number of production workers in a computerized, low-noise environment.[11] Technology has been the main cause of the reduced number of jobs in manufacturing. Moreover, many jobs lost in factories have simply been relabeled as belonging to service industries because they have been outsourced to specialized firms—maintenance, cafeteria, logistics, or marketing jobs, for example. Another sort of false job loss may lie in the statistical reclassification of former manufacturing firms as nonmanufacturing firms even though they have maintained their conception, engineering, coordination, and distribution activities.[12]

Comparative Advantage Has Shifted

The cost of iPads and iPhones illustrates the changes that have occurred in manufacturing and supply chains. Half a dozen years ago, manufacturing costs (manufacturing in the sense of assembling) already accounted for only 1–2 percent of the price of these devices. The rest of the costs went to conception, engineering, software, design, and marketing, which were mostly provided in the United States. Between half and two-thirds of the consumer price of these devices remained in the United States. This example suggests that the trade deficit may be exaggerated in official statistics.[13]

With these developments, comparative advantage has shifted. Developing countries now have a comparative advantage in assembling components, which requires a lot of unspecialized labor. The comparative advantage of the United States lies in the more high-end services—such as conception, design, engineering, logistics, and distribution—not in manufacturing itself.

A Misleading Objection

It is thus misleading to say that the United States is losing its factories. What is happening is that factories have changed, and the United Sates now has a comparative advantage only in the most advanced manufacturing activities. This is not deindustrialization but rather the birth of a new configuration of manufacturing. The old manufacturing jobs for low-skilled workers have disappeared and will not come back unless the world gets much poorer. As the *Economist* explains, "Politicians cannot bring back old-fashioned factory jobs."[14]

In this context, protectionism for the manufacturing industry is a Luddite resistance to change. Economist David Dollar writes that "'protectionism' is an aptly chosen word as it aims to lock in place an old industrial structure, rather than helping workers and communities adjust to inevitable change."[15] Americans should embrace economic progress, as they are used to doing. There is nothing magical about old-style manufacturing. Physical things continue to be produced, but production occurs more efficiently—that is, it uses fewer resources. There is no reason why the state should protect manufacturing, especially obsolete manufacturing. Andrew B. Bernard, Valerie Smeets, and Frederic Warzynski note that protecting manufacturing has been a standard component of industrial policy.[16] They report that in 2012, the French government created a ministry for "industrial recovery."[17] There is no reason the US government should imitate this sort of policy. Free markets and free trade are better solutions than protectionist planning by politicians and bureaucrats. Free trade increases consumption possibilities—that is, the standard of living. In the next chapter, we will see how free trade also boosts economic growth—that is, the rate of increase in the standard of living over time.

ESSAY 4: THE NEW MANUFACTURING AND THE AMERICAN ECONOMY

Over the last several decades, consumer demand has grown mainly in services (education, healthcare, housing, recreation, etc.) rather than in food or physical objects. In international trade, America's comparative advantage has also shifted toward services such as travel (including travel for education- and health-related purposes), intellectual property, transportation, finance and insurance, and other business services. As a consequence, many manufacturing jobs have moved to services.

Figure 4.1 shows how the number of manufacturing jobs in the United States has been declining, from its peak of more than 19 million jobs in 1979 to about 12 million in 2016, although the scale of the graph makes it difficult to see clearly. Over the same period, total employment (the total number of employed people in the civilian sector) has grown continuously, from about 99 million to more than 151 million—a growth of 53 percent in less than half a century. In other words, much more jobs have been created in the whole economy than have disappeared in manufacturing. This has been a general trend in advanced countries.[18]

The number of jobs or employed people is a poor metric of welfare because it takes into account neither worker productivity nor the value of leisure to most individuals. If workers are more productive, the average incomes (and presumably the welfare) of everybody, including of those who don't work, will be higher, other things being equal. With high labor productivity, students don't have to work (at least not full-time) because their parents (or the taxpayers)

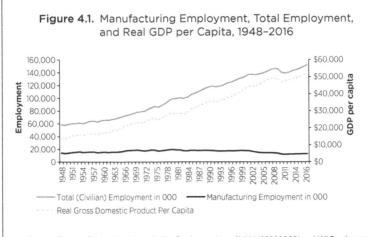

Figure 4.1. Manufacturing Employment, Total Employment, and Real GDP per Capita, 1948–2016

—— Total (Civilian) Employment in 000   ━━ Manufacturing Employment in 000
- - - Real Gross Domestic Product Per Capita

Sources: Bureau of Labor Statistics, "Civilian Employment Level" (LNU02000000) and "All Employees: Manufacturing" (CEU3000000001); Bureau of Economic Analysis, "Gross Domestic Product Per Capita (A939RX0Q048SBEA). Retrieved from FRED Economic Data, Federal Reserve Bank of St. Louis, July 27, 2017, https://fred.stlouisfed.org/.

can help them; similarly, the retired can afford not to work because they have earned enough during their working lives. And individuals who prefer more leisure instead of more consumption are able to make this choice at lower cost.

A better metric of welfare is real GDP per capita, which indicates the volume of goods and services available to the average person in the economy. GDP per capita is also equal to total average income over the whole economy. Figure 4.1 shows that real GDP per capita has grown continually (except temporarily during recessions). Since 1979, the peak of manufacturing employment, real GDP has increased from $28,725 per American resident to $51,523, a growth of 79 percent—more than employment, demonstrating the impact of productivity growth. The net effect of economic change has been a higher value of goods and services available to the average American.

The growth in the total number of jobs combined with the reduction of employment in manufacturing implies that the percentage of employment in manufacturing has been trending downward. Using the numbers underlying figure 4.1, the ratio of manufacturing employment to total employment in the American economy has decreased from more than 25 percent in the early 1950s to 8 percent today.

The emblematic closing of Youngstown Sheet and Tube Company in Youngstown, Ohio, on September 19, 1977, exemplified these trends.[19] But the long erosion of total employment in manufacturing (since the late 1970s) and relative employment in manufacturing (since the early 1950s) does not mean that manufacturing output has declined in an absolute sense. On the contrary, because of the productivity increase, real manufacturing output itself continued to grow until the start of the Great Recession.

Figure 4.2 shows this in two ways. The solid line depicts an index of manufacturing production from 1972 to 2016 in constant dollars (meaning that the impact of inflation has been subtracted, leaving only real production). Real manufacturing production increased by 180 percent—it nearly tripled—between 1972 and its peak in 2007, just before the Great Recession. From there, it dropped by 18 percent in two years, but has been recovering since then. In 2016, it is still 4 percent below its 2007 peak.

A better measure of manufacturing output is real value added—that is, total production minus intermediate inputs. Value added is the same as contribution to GDP (which is the sum of all values added). The dashed line in figure 4.2 follows value added in manufacturing since 1997, the first year for which this statistic is available. This line confirms the growth of manufacturing until 2007, and suggests that

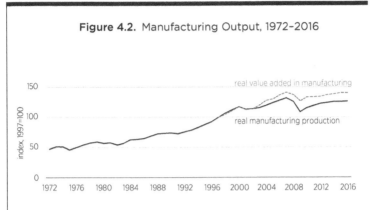

Figure 4.2. Manufacturing Output, 1972–2016

Sources: Real manufacturing production: Board of Governors of the Federal Reserve System (US), "Industrial Production: Manufacturing (NAICS)" (IPGMFNQ), retrieved from FRED Economic Data, Federal Reserve Bank of St. Louis, July 14, 2017, https://fred.stlouisfed.org/, rebased to 1997 by author. Real value added in manufacturing: Bureau of Economic Analysis, "Chain-Type Quantity Indexes for Value Added by Industry," April 21, 2017, rebased to 1997 dollars by author.

manufacturing has nearly completely recovered from the recession—it is only 1 percent lower than the 2007 peak. Value added in manufacturing is up 40 percent since 1997.

According to both measures of output—production and value added—it appears that manufacturing output has either plateaued or is poised to continue its growth after the recession dip. Only the future will tell, but we know that technology has dramatically increased labor's productivity and allowed larger real manufacturing output with fewer workers. Many more jobs have been created in other sectors than have disappeared in manufacturing. And the value added, or GDP, or total income created in manufacturing has not decreased.

CHAPTER 5

Objection: Trade Destroys Jobs

The argument that trade destroys jobs is based on the notion that anything imported into the United States is not made here as it would otherwise have been. This lower domestic production implies that less labor is used. Imports therefore destroy American jobs. Of course, the exports made possible by free trade require more American labor, but these jobs do not completely replace the ones lost to imports, for two reasons. First, the current trade deficit means that net jobs are destroyed. Second, exports may come from more capital-intensive or technology-intensive sectors of the economy while imports replace mainly labor-intensive goods; so, on balance, jobs are lost.

Despite its apparent plausibility, economic analysis shows that this argument is not compelling.

Jobs vs. Consumption

The number of jobs is not a satisfactory metric of incomes or welfare.[1] People produce in order to consume, not the other way around. Faced with the choice between working for an income or obtaining an equal (or even a lower) income without having to work, most people would choose the latter. The purpose of work is mainly to obtain an income and, even more fundamentally, the increased welfare that income makes possible. It is true that the typical individual is both a consumer and a producer, and most people need a job to earn an income, but the goal is consumption, not sweat.[2] Thus, consumption and the incomes necessary to consume are better indicators of welfare than is the number of jobs.

This approach does take into account the noneconomic aspects of jobs. For many people, part of their job is a consumption good—in terms of dignity or self-reliance, for example—but this component would be an insufficient incentive to hold the job if an income did not also come with it. It is presumably more the income and independence a job provides than the actual work done that contribute to the sense of dignity. Many observations are consistent with this hypothesis. When remuneration decreases, the quantity of labor supplied generally diminishes; economists say that the labor supply curve has a positive slope.[3] Casey Mulligan, a University of Chicago economist, calculates that half the depression of the labor market during the 2008–2009 recession came from the incentives created by the expansion of the safety net.[4] Gallup's "State of the American Workplace" surveys estimate that one-third of US employees are "engaged" with their jobs ("involved in, enthusiastic"), suggesting that two-thirds are there only for the paycheck.[5]

Net Jobs Are Not Destroyed

Trade may resemble technological progress, which eliminates jobs in some sectors but creates an equivalent or higher number of jobs elsewhere in the economy. The advance of technology in manufacturing over the past few decades can serve as an illustration. The decline in the number of manufacturing jobs due to technology has not resulted in a net loss, because the increased incomes generated by higher productivity have led to the creation of an equivalent (in fact slightly higher) number of jobs in other sectors, as shown by David Autor of MIT and Anna Salomons of the Utrecht University School of Economics. Using a dataset covering 19 countries (the United States, Japan, and several Western European countries) over 37 years (1970–2007), Autor and Salomons confirm that technological progress has raised labor productivity and reduced jobs in the sectors directly affected, but find that the resulting higher incomes generated offsetting jobs in other industries. Autor and Salomons conclude that "productivity growth has been employment-augmenting rather than employment-reducing."[6]

Trade should produce the same result. As we saw, trade increases real incomes, that is, consumption possibilities—through the working of comparative advantage—so it must also increase job opportunities. This assumes of course that some individuals want to work more; some may prefer the opportunity of more leisure. But there is no reason to think that trade would reduce job opportunities for someone who wants to work or work more.

Short-Run Costs

Shifts in competition, trade, or comparative advantage can bring disruptions that result in job losses. A study by David Autor, David Dorn, and Gordon Hanson emphasized the effect on employment of what they refer to as the "China shock,"[7] that is, the growth of Chinese manufacturing exports, especially in the 1999–2011 period. This shock adversely affected some manufacturing sectors throughout the developed world—furniture, textiles, apparel, electronic devices, appliances, and so forth. The econometric estimates of Autor and his colleagues (including those from previous work with Daron Acemoglu and Brendan

Price) indicate that, of the 5.8 million manufacturing jobs that were lost in the 1999–2011 period, about 1.0 million were lost directly or indirectly because of the China shock; and that, adding indirect effects on other industries and "aggregate demand" effects, perhaps as many as 2.4 million jobs were lost in the whole economy. The researchers calculated that a large number of individuals who lost their manufacturing jobs to the China shock were not able to find new jobs or had to accept new ones with lower wages. Relatively few switched industries or moved to other regions. In other words, labor markets have been much less flexible than expected, which brought high adjustment costs.

As mentioned by Autor, Dorn, and Hanson, government assistance programs—including Trade Adjustment Assistance and unemployment benefits, but mainly general assistance programs such as healthcare and disability benefits—presented perverse incentives to workers displaced by Chinese imports. Growing regulation should also be considered a factor in labor market inflexibility, including occupational licensure and minimum wages and European-flavored regulation of labor contracts. It thus appears that market inflexibility was the problem, not trade as such. This is where, it would seem, solutions should be found.

Autor, Dorn, and Hanson may have overestimated the problem, as a paper by economist Jonathan Rothwell suggested.[8] However, this critique has been rejected by Autor, Dorn, and Hanson.[9] The controversy appears to be partly about the econometrics involved. At any rate, Rothwell points out that foreign competition has effects similar to those of domestic competition and that it is not clear why we should protect workers from the former more than from the latter.

Technological change—not international trade—drove most of the reduction in manufacturing jobs. Even according to Autor, Dorn, and Hanson's high estimate, most of the decline in manufacturing jobs is not explained by the China shock. Michael

Hicks and Srikant Devaraj calculate that between 2000 and 2010, only one in 10 manufacturing job losses in the United States is attributable to trade, compared with nine in 10 caused by productivity gains (that is, technological change).[10] The McKinsey Global Institute estimates that 20 percent of the job losses in US manufacturing during the 2000–2010 period were caused by trade, including offshoring.[11] Another study calculates that less than 20 percent of the decline of manufacturing employment between 1970 and 1994 in 18 industrial countries was caused by trade between developed and poor countries.[12]

Some six million *net* jobs (after deducting the losses in manufacturing) were created in America during the China-shock period (1999–2011), despite the most serious recession since the Great Depression.[13] It should also be remembered that about 10 percent of Americans are employed in goods-producing industries—agriculture, mining, and manufacturing—the sectors that mainly produce traded goods.[14] Consequently, the potential for disruption by trade remains limited. It is true that imports of services have increased, but the American economy has a comparative advantage in those (see essay 1).

It is noteworthy that Autor, Dorn, and Hanson do not seem to question the long-term benefits of free trade. Consumers who benefit from lower prices must gain more than producers lose in the outcompeted industries. Because of poor labor mobility, this net benefit may take many years to overcome short-run adjustment costs, but there will eventually be net benefits.[15]

The China shock is probably over because Chinese wages have increased and other poor countries (including Bangladesh, Vietnam, and Thailand) have become new destinations for the outsourcing of old-style manufacturing. "The great China trade experiment may soon be over," write Autor, Dorn, and Hanson, "if it is not already. The country is moving beyond the period of catch-up associated with its market transition and becoming a middle income nation."[16] (If China returns to unabashed author-itarianism, moreover, it will likely lose some, perhaps much, of its economic efficiency.) It is interesting to note that in the 1980s, the big scare was Japan, and it was greatly exaggerated. The chief executive of Intel predicted that the United States would become a "techno-colony of Japan."[17]

Although one may sympathize with the victims of economic disruptions, trade should not be impeded any more than techno-logical progress just because of its short-run costs. Nassau Senior, a well-known 19th-century British economist, already saw the problem:

> If we should think it madness to prohibit, or to tax, the use of an improved steam-engine, because it must be injurious to those employed in raising coal, what pretence is there for prohibiting or taxing foreign ribands or velvets because their importation would be injurious to the English silk-weaver? . . .
>
> . . . To prohibit every change which is accompanied by individual injury would be to prohibit every improvement whatever.[18]

Long-Term and Dynamic Benefits of International Trade

The impact of trade on future economic growth must be fac-tored into the calculation of trade's benefits and costs. A num-ber of empirical studies have concluded that openness to trade is associated with higher rates of economic growth.[19] Economic theory supports the idea that international trade carries dynamic benefits over and above those suggested by the static law of com-parative advantage—that is, trade not only has a one-shot, level effect on GDP per capita, but it also increases the future rate of growth. The possible channels by which trade can boost the rate of economic growth are many. Trade can increase the volume and quality of capital via imports of capital goods; it can fuel technological progress through the same channel and through the general diffusion of knowledge. Growing competition at the world level constantly challenges producers to become more efficient.[20] Openness to the world promotes better institutions through imitation. Local corruption is rendered more difficult by the option of exporting capital. Trade also allows businesses to gain economies of scale by extending their markets. This last observation brings exports back into the argument for free trade. As Adam Smith observed, the extent of the market facilitates the division of labor.[21]

Protectionism, on the contrary, is more likely to dampen growth. It reduces the incentives of domestic firms and limits the extent of their market. A traditional protectionist argument, often called the "infant industry" argument, claims that certain industries require temporary protection until they have had enough time to match the efficiency of foreign producers. In reality, these protected industries tend to remain infants forever because the producers have no incentive to become more productive. The beneficiaries of protectionism seldom claim that they have outgrown the need for it. For example, most of the US textile and apparel industry, despite major protection from the late 1960s until 2005, could not be maintained artificially; other developed countries had the same experience. The American steel industry has been protected for decades (in fact, it was protected during the 19th century too), and it is still asking for protection. At any rate, the return on investment in an infant industry should be high enough to make up for the losses incurred while it was becoming profitable—but if this were the case it could obtain financing from private investors and would not need protection.

Amazon, which has yet to pay a dividend, does not need government protection, because investors expect the company to remunerate their patience appropriately in the future.[22]

Some empirical studies have questioned the positive link between economic growth and openness to trade. For example, Prabirjit Sarkar, who used panel data for a sample of 51 less developed countries (LDCs) over the period 1961–2002, found that only the richest and most trade-dependent LDCs showed a positive relationship between international trade and growth.[23] Sarkar claimed that an "editorial bias" explains the "mainstream" academic consensus in favor of a positive link.[24] Despite this claim, the debate seems to revolve around the proper econometric models to use for estimating the relationship between openness to trade and economic growth, and whether their results can be interpreted as a causal relationship or merely as correlation.[25]

In general, however, the empirical evidence broadly confirms the growth effects of openness to international trade. After reviewing the economic research and debates over the past decades, Romain Wacziarg and Karen Horn Welch analyze data from a sample of 133 countries between 1950 and 1998.[26] They conclude that "countries that liberalized their trade regimes experienced average annual growth rates that were about 1.5 percentage points higher than before liberalization."[27] After pointing out some limitations of existing econometric estimates and the existence of other conditions for developing countries to benefit from openness, two other economists, Lill Andersen and Ronald Babula, conclude,

> Is there a link between openness and growth? Based on this survey of the most recent empirical and theoretical literature, we believe that the answer is yes. Nearly all empirical analyses confirm this.[28]

Liberalization of trade appears to have been a major factor in the rapid development of many countries that were very poor a few decades ago. In many economies, rapid development depended on trade liberalization; in others, trade liberalization was accompanied by internal liberalization. The two effects are not easy to separate, but according to Wacziarg and Horn Welch, trade has often been the main contributor to higher economic growth.[29] Paul Krugman and his coauthors note,

> Beginning in the mid-1980s, a number of developing countries moved to lower tariff rates and removed import quotas and other restrictions to trade. The shift of developing countries toward free trade is the big trade policy story of the past two and a half decades. . . . The old view that import substitution is the only path to development has been proven wrong, as a number of developing countries have achieved extraordinary growth while becoming more, not less, open to trade.[30]

Conclusion and Another Objection

To summarize the problems with the job-loss objection to free trade, three lessons from economics are relevant. First, jobs are a poor metric for the welfare of individuals. The objective for most, if not all, individuals is not to work, but to obtain income with which to consume and otherwise pursue their own welfare. It is because free trade benefits consumers that economists consider it efficient. A growing, efficient economy requires consumer sovereignty, not domination by producers. Second, although changes in technology and comparative advantage do generate adjustment costs in terms of gross job losses (especially in times of rapid technological change), the job opportunities and the *net* number of available jobs do not decrease with trade. Employment opportunities are a reflection of growing income, and trade increases income. Third, we must also consider the dynamic benefits of free trade. Free trade promotes future growth. More growth means more job opportunities and, depending on one's preferences, more leisure.

At this point, protectionists usually offer a counter-objection. People's activities as producers may well be subordinate to their activities as consumers, but individuals without a job cannot consume, even if they get good prices from China. This counter-objection neglects two considerations. First, there is no way to have an economic system where the producer is protected from consumers by barriers to trade while the consumer is protected from producers by competition. Competition and barriers to trade are as antithetical at the international level as they are at the domestic level.

Ultimately, either the consumer or the producer is running the system. Consumers can't benefit from competitive prices while producers are protected against competitive challenges. Second, theory and experience show that an economy where the consumer is sovereign satisfies individual preferences better than a system in which producers rule by vying for privileges from the state.

ESSAY 5: JOBS, JOBS, JOBS, AND ECONOMIC GROWTH

When people say that what is needed is "jobs, jobs, jobs," what they really mean is incomes and consumption possibilities. Now, free trade, not protectionism, is the way to maximize incomes and consumption possibilities.

Protectionism can protect jobs, but these jobs are the ones that should disappear because they cannot be maintained by free consumer choice. One example among many was provided by the increased tariffs on imports of Chinese tires imposed by President Barack Obama in 2009. One estimate puts the cost to consumers in increased prices at $900,000 per year for each job saved in the domestic tire industry. This amount equals 22 times the average wages of those whose jobs were saved. Moreover, because individuals and businesses had to pay more for tires and thus buy less of other things, jobs were destroyed elsewhere in the economy: it is estimated that the number of jobs lost was three times larger than the number of tire jobs protected—so that the *net* number of jobs in the economy *decreased* by 2,531.[31] In the net, protectionism destroys jobs because it stifles efficient production and the generation of incomes.

Trade Promotes Economic Growth, Which Generates Jobs

Besides the static benefits of comparative advantage, trade has dynamic advantages. Free trade increases the rate of GDP growth or, what is the same, the growth of total incomes over time. One econometric study estimates that between 1950 and 1998, "countries that liberalized their trade regimes experienced average annual growth rates that were about 1.5 percentage points higher than before liberalization."[32]

As an illustration, figure 5.1 plots annual GDP growth against reductions in average tariff rates for 46 countries (both advanced economies and emerging or developing economies for which consistent data exist) between 1990 and 2015. A positive correlation is clearly visible on the chart: the larger the reduction in tariffs, the higher the rate economic growth. (Correlation is not causation, but it provides a confirmation of causation when theory predicts a causal

Figure 5.1. Changes in Average Tariff and Annual GDP Growth, 1990–2015

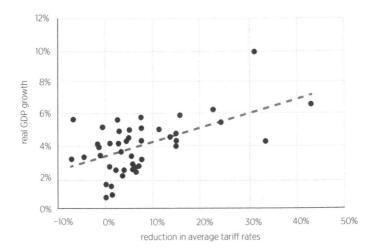

Note: The 46 countries comprise developing economies, emerging markets, and advanced economies for which consistent data exist in International Monetary Fund databases. A negative reduction means an increase in tariffs.
Source: International Monetary Fund, World Bank, and World Trade Organization, "Making Trade an Engine of Growth for All: The Case for Trade and for Policies to Facilitate Adjustment," April 10, 2017, p. 9.

relationship.) Formal tariffs, of course, don't tell the whole story—nontariff measures also exist. But the chart illustrates the general point that free trade is favorable to economic growth.

The Number of Gross Jobs Lost to Trade Is Tiny

To put in perspective the job losses attributed to trade, consider the following statistics. Between 1999 and 2011, a period covering the so-called China shock, 5.8 million manufacturing jobs disappeared, and at most 2.4 million jobs were lost in the whole economy because of imports from China.[33] This number is small in comparison to the normal churn (destruction and creation) of jobs in the American economy. During the China shock period, 13.4 million jobs were created *every year* on average and 13.1 million destroyed (for a net gain of about 300,000 per year, unusually low because of the Great Recession). In a dynamic economy, jobs are continuously destroyed and replaced by new, more numerous jobs. A look at the recent numbers confirm this picture, but with more job creations. Over a 12-month period from March 2016 to March 2017, 12.9 million new private jobs were created and 10.9 million disappeared, for a net two million jobs created annually. Since 2011, nearly as many new private jobs are created on net every year in America as manufacturing jobs were lost over 12 years owing to the China shock (2.4 million), and this is not an unusual situation.[34]

Jobs Are Mainly Related to Population Growth

Economists David Autor and Anna Salomons note that productivity has been a minor factor in employment changes, because the main factor in job creation is simply population growth.[35] They could have related this to Say's law: supply creates its own demand. New workers arriving in the labor force generate a demand for goods and services equivalent to their own production, because this demand is the very reason why they work and produce.[36] The same point can be made about trade: population rather than trade drives employment. Free trade that follows comparative advantage, however, leads to more valuable production and larger incomes.

The fact that the number of jobs basically follows the evolution of population is illustrated by figure 5.2, which

Figure 5.2. Working-Age Population and Employment in the United States, 1960–2016

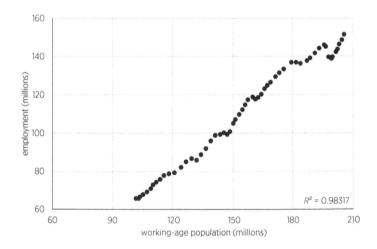

$R^2 = 0.98317$

Source: Bureau of Labor Statistics, "Civilian Employment Level" (LNU02000000), data retrieved from FRED Economic Data, Federal Reserve Bank of St. Louis, August 10, 2017, https://fred.stlouisfed.org /series/LNU02000000. Organization for Economic Co-operation and Development, "Working Age Population: Aged 15–64: All Persons for the United States" (LFWA64TTUSQ647N), data retrieved from FRED Economic Data, Federal Reserve Bank of St. Louis, August 10, 2017, https://fred.stlouisfed .org/series/LFWA64TTUSQ647N.

shows the level of civilian employment in relation to the American working-age population (15 to 64 years of age). Each dot represents one year between 1960 and 2016. The evolution of employment closely tracks the evolution of the working-age population. The coefficient of correlation is close to unity, indicating a very high correlation, and is highly statistically significant, meaning that it is not due to chance. (Because working population (and employment) increases with time, the horizontal axis nearly coincides with chronological dates. The drop in the employment toward the end of the curve corresponds to the 2008–2009 recession.)

Benefits to Consumers, Especially the Poor

Benefit to consumers is what matters. People with lower budgets spend proportionately more on internationally traded goods such as manufactured goods and agricultural goods. Higher-income earners, on the contrary, spend proportionately more on goods that are not generally traded, such as education, health, and housing. One would thus expect trade to benefit the poor more than the middle class, and the middle class more than the rich. Some evidence supports this hypothesis. Pablo Fajgelbaum of the University of California, Los Angeles, and Amit Khandelwal of Columbia University have developed a model by which they estimate that the American consumer at the 10th percentile in the revenue distribution owes 69 percent of his or her purchasing power to international trade, the median consumer (at the 50th percentile) 37 percent, and the consumer at the 90th percentile only 4 percent. As an illustration of the importance of trade, one can think of these estimates as representing the real income losses that would be suffered if

American borders were completely closed to international trade.[37] Research by the US International Trade Commission about the impact of trade agreements "suggests that U.S. consumers who are either middle income (income between $40,000 and $69,000) or lower income (income less than $40,000) benefit disproportionately from the savings associated with the tariff reductions."[38]

Protectionism does not create net jobs, or it can only create wasteful jobs—jobs that waste resources. Jobs are the way people earn incomes in order to consume more (more goods or more leisure) and to maximize their welfare. Just like domestic trade, free international trade contributes to maximizing income, to consumption opportunities, and to "the pursuit of happiness."

CHAPTER 6

Objection: Trade Lowers Wages

Besides the problems of inflexible labor markets and job losses (discussed in the previous chapter), another objection is that free trade with poor or developing countries pushes down wages in rich countries such as the United States. This alleged effect is sometimes referred to as the *pauper labor argument*, and it seems to make sense at first sight. If American workers compete (indirectly, through their employers) with Chinese workers to manufacture textiles, will this not push American workers' wages down? Expanding the supply of labor—even indirectly—lowers wages, other things being equal.

But other things are not equal, and economic analysis suggests that, in general, trade does not reduce real wages—"real wages" meaning what a worker can buy in goods and services with his wages. On the contrary, for the reasons already considered, trade should reduce the prices of consumer goods, and increase the average US resident's real income, compared to what they would be without trade.

Wages Are Determined by Productivity

In a poor country, the generally lower labor productivity translates into low average wages. In a rich country, labor's generally higher productivity brings higher average wages. Indeed, we empirically observe that wages vary with productivity: for example, the Philippines, China, and Mexico have, compared with the United States, wage rates that are proportional to their relative productivity.[1] According to the theory of comparative advantage, trade will increase labor productivity because workers will work in the most productive industries. Moreover, the dynamic advantages of free trade should boost economic growth. Thus, the average labor productivity and the level of wages will rise. This reasoning can be expressed as a syllogism: wages are determined by labor productivity; free trade increases labor productivity; therefore, free trade increases wages.

Trade and the Distribution of Income

One factor could reduce real wages, or at least slow their rise in the course of economic growth. Two Swedish economists, Eli Heckscher and Bertil Ohlin, demonstrated in the early 20th century that a country's comparative advantage will attach to the goods that use relatively more of its most abundant factor of production and that are therefore less expensive to produce.[2] Imagine a country that has more capital (in the form of computers, equipment, laboratories, and so forth) and less labor compared with another that has more labor and less capital. The first country could be America, the second China. When the two countries trade with each other, America will export capital-intensive goods (such as airliners or microchips) and import labor-intensive goods (such as appliances assembled in Chinese labor-intensive factories). Thus, American demand will increase the price of labor in China, and

Chinese demand will push up the price of capital goods in America. But American wages will decrease because American workers now compete with Chinese labor, and the price of Chinese capital goods, which face the competition of American capital, will fall. However, Heckscher and Ohlin recognized that the *real* wages of American labor will increase because American workers will now be able to buy more goods and services, which have become less expensive. Think about appliances and furniture, for example, whose prices have been brought down by imports from China (see essay 8). This leads to the same conclusion as before: trade will increase the real wages of American workers.[3]

Not a Zero-Sum Game

The argument always comes back to the benefits of exchange and to comparative advantage (augmented by economic growth). Exchange between two individuals is not a zero-sum game: there is not one winner and one loser. Both parties gain something—otherwise, one of the parties would have declined the exchange. In the same way, international trade is not a zero-sum game: both countries gain. For each country, the benefits are higher than the costs. This is true for two reasons. First, each individual importer or exporter gains; otherwise, one would have declined to pursue the exchange. Therefore, because countries are made up of individuals, each country gains. Second, overall benefits exceed overall costs, even counting the costs of third parties such as producers put out of business or workers who lose their jobs. Trade can change the distribution of income (the size of individual slices of pie), but it produces more real income (the pie as a whole gets bigger).[4]

One of the benefits of international trade that we tend to forget is the increase in competition it brings to domestic markets. Such competition pushes prices down and thus increases real wages. Some people have expressed concern about the increased business concentration in America, and some data seem to support them.[5] An easy solution is simply to open the borders wider to foreign competition—in commercial flights and cabotage, for example.

To summarize, trade will not, except under exceptional or transitory circumstances, lower real wages. In an advanced economy such as that of the United States, trade does increase the competition faced by unspecialized labor, which is relatively scarce. (On the other hand, skilled labor and capital are relatively plentiful and will be more in demand.) But free trade simultaneously increases labor productivity and total consumption because of the benefits of comparative advantage and economic growth. US workers benefit from lower prices for their consumption goods, raising their real wages and salaries. We can expect trade to increase real income for most people and most workers.

ESSAY 6: LABOR PRODUCTIVITY AND REMUNERATION

Free international trade increases labor productivity and thus raises wages. Greater productivity means higher wages because employers bid up the price of more productive labor. This theoretical prediction is confirmed by figure 6.1, which shows that wages across countries (shown here as proportions of American wages) are roughly proportional to the countries' labor productivity (measured in proportion to US labor productivity).[6]

Poor countries are poor because their workers earn little, and their workers earn little because they are relatively

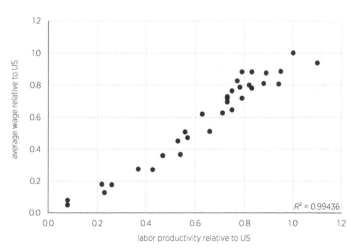

Figure 6.1. Labor Productivity and Wages in 33 Countries, 2000

$R^2 = 0.99436$

labor productivity relative to US

Source: Kathryn G. Marshall, "International Productivity and Factor Price Comparisons," *Journal of International Economics* 87 (2012).

unproductive. When free trade increases labor productivity, it also raises workers' incomes and the general income level in the country.

In America (and, in general, in other developed countries), labor market polarization has been more a problem of education than a problem of international competition. Figure 6.2 shows the evolution of median earnings among employees as a function of educational achievement in America. These data confirm the widely documented phenomenon that technological progress has polarized the labor market, separating the more educated, who can more easily learn new skills, from the less educated, who are left behind. Since 1979 (the first year for which these data are available), the median weekly earnings of college graduates have grown faster than the median weekly earnings of those

Figure 6.2. Median Weekly Earnings by Educational Attainment, 1979–2016

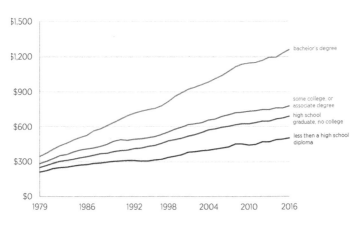

Source: Bureau of Labor Statistics, Weekly and Hourly Earnings Data from the Current Population Survey, series LEU0252916700, LEU0252917300, LEU0254929400, LEU0252918500.

who have only a high school diploma or some college,[7] and even faster than the earnings of those who did not obtain a high school diploma (increases, respectively, of 266 percent, about 177 percent, and 140 percent).

If we consider the real earnings (in constant dollars, that is, taking out the impact of price inflation) of the median employee, only workers with a bachelor's degree or a higher degree have benefited from an increase in earnings since 1979, according to data from the Bureau of Labor Statistics.[8] Note, however, that the bureau's definition of "weekly earnings" excludes income from self-employment, second jobs, employee-paid fringe benefits, and government transfers.

This evolution of relative wages and salaries is consistent with an increased demand for highly skilled workers. In the typical advanced country since the mid-1970s, employment of skilled labor has outstripped employment of less-skilled labor. (In America, untypically, those at the bottom of the skill ladder have also seen a high demand for their services, the middle-skilled being the ones who have apparently faced slower-growing employment.)[9]

The polarization of the labor market has been caused primarily by technological progress, and it will last until the less-educated learn the skills they need in order to adapt to a high-tech economy. Protectionism would only pull most people's real incomes down, including those of the poorest, who are likely to benefit most from the price reductions caused by imports, as suggested in essay 5.

CHAPTER 7

The Politics of Trade and a Bit More Economics

Now comes the puzzle: If free trade is so beneficial, why has protectionist sentiment remained alive and well in government circles and in most historical periods? Why is it so difficult to reduce barriers to international trade?

Protectionism in the Real Political World

The answer is that, in political reality, protectionism does not aim to maximize income or welfare but to protect the special interests of certain producers. Even if free trade benefits consumers across the board, it hurts some producers' interests. Protectionism has the opposite effect—it hurts most people but benefits special interests among producers. Why do special interests win against the interests of most people, and why are policies enacted if they have higher costs than benefits? These phenomena are explained by what economists call the *theory of collective action*: small, concentrated interests have greater ability and incentives to organize for lobbying and other political action than large, diffuse interests do. In general, the better-organized and better-financed interests win in the political process.[1]

Sugar protection in the United States provides a good example of the effects of collective action. Imports of sugar are restricted by an import quota, which is equivalent to a tariff in that it increases the domestic price. The price of sugar in the United States much exceeds the world price—by 52 percent in 2016 (which is still below the average premium Americans have had to pay in the past). This protection is estimated to cost American consumers $4.4 billion per year, or $30 for the average household. Most individuals will think saving that amount of money for their families is not worth the trouble of getting organized and contributing to lobbying and political campaigns. On the other hand, a small number of domestic farmers and large processors and refiners (who own several of the foreign sugar exporters that benefit from the higher prices in the American market) gain about $3.9 billion a year owing to the import quota. (The difference of $500 million represents most of the net cost of protectionism in the sugar market.) This small group of producers has a strong incentive to lobby for the quota. Indeed, they contributed more than $4.5 million to the 2012 congressional election, and the American Sugar Alliance spent $3 million more just before the quota was reauthorized in 2013.[2]

The steel industry is representative of protectionism in many respects. In the United States, iron and then steel were protected by tariffs during most of the 19th century. Economist Frank Taussig reported that, around 1880, a steel tariff of about 100 percent pushed the price of rails in the United States to twice the price in England.[3] This price disparity should come as no surprise: raising domestic prices is the purpose of a tariff. A tariff is a tax on domestic consumers. During the first decades of the 20th century, steel tariffs were reduced to around 35 percent. After a lull in the middle of the century, steel protectionism was revived in the 1970s and 1980s when quotas limited steel imports from Japan and Europe. Since then, antidumping cases brought by steel companies have been the main protectionist tool. As of June 28, 2017, the US government has 402 antidumping and countervailing duties in place, more than half of which hit iron and steel. As trade economist Douglas Irwin writes, "The steel industry has received nearly continuous protection for over thirty years and is still seeking limits on imports."[4]

Special interests' requests for protection are often phrased in terms of defending the public interest against "market failures" (situations in which markets cannot efficiently satisfy consumer demand).[5] There is no reason to believe that more market failures occur in international trade than in domestic trade. But even if, in special circumstances, a convincing case could be made for market failure, there is no reason to believe that politicians and bureaucrats (who, in practice, run the government) could provide an efficient solution. Even if those individuals were perfectly well intentioned, they are not omniscient and cannot comprehend the detailed complexity of the economy. They lack local knowledge about consumer preferences and the costs and opportunities of producers. This "knowledge problem" has been well explained by F. A. Hayek, the winner of the 1974 Nobel Prize in economics.[6] There is no reason to believe that government can efficiently calculate, impose, and enforce optimal tariffs. Political failures are likely to be more damaging than any market failure, as shown by historical attempts to plan and control economies.

Domestic and International Trade

For individuals, the benefits of exchange cut across political borders—they are not confined within a country. If free trade between the United States and Mexico is detrimental, it should also be detrimental between California and Mississippi. Average wages are 40 percent lower in Mississippi than in California.[7] A protectionist would not understand how California's producers could compete with Mississippi's. Why don't Californians import all their goods from Mississippi? (The answer, as the reader will understand by now, lies in the theory of comparative advantage.) On the other side of the bad deal, the protectionist argument would also claim that the rich California-based company Uber disrupts poor taxicab drivers in Mississippi and kills their jobs. Are both California and Mississippi exploited by free trade between the two states? Of course not. Free trade between Californians and Mississippians benefits consumers in both states. But if the arguments for protectionism between California and Mississippi are invalid, they must also be false at the international level.

A typical protectionist will retort that free trade among countries is different. But why would that be the case? Protectionism against foreigners amounts to a coercive redistribution among the citizens allegedly "protected"—a coercive redistribution analogous to what would be the consequences of forbidding California consumers to buy from Mississippi producers, thereby redistributing income from California consumers to California producers. In the 1870s, congressman Samuel Cox (D-NY) understood that protectionism favors parts of the country at the expense of other parts. As he put it, protectionism steals from consumers from somewhere in the country to give to producers elsewhere. He sarcastically declared,

Let us be to each other instruments of reciprocal rapine. Michigan steals on copper; Maine on lumber; Pennsylvania on iron; North Carolina on peanuts; Massachusetts on cotton goods; Connecticut on hair pins; New Jersey on spool thread; Louisiana on sugar, and so on. Why not let the gentleman from Maryland steal coal from them? True, but a comparative few get the benefit, and it comes out of the body of the people.[8]

The justification for opposing international trade while allowing domestic trade may also come from a nationalist ideology that aims to force all citizens into the same mold under the state. Jawaharlal Nehru, prime minister of India from 1947 to 1964, illustrated the protectionist power of the nationalist ideology when he said, "I believe, as a practical proposition, that it is better to have a second rate thing made in our country, than a first rate thing that one has to import."[9] Nehru presumably was not expressing a purely personal preference (which would be strange but permissible); he was expressing the will to coerce a number of Indians into following his own preferences.

It should be noted that free trade is a substitute for immigration—not a perfect substitute, but a substitute nonetheless. It provides foreign workers with economic opportunities as exporters while they remain in their often-preferred social environment. Free trade also enables Americans (or citizens of other rich countries) to benefit from inexpensive foreign labor without what some view as immigration costs.

To summarize this chapter, the politics of trade naturally tends toward protectionism. Free trade is often viewed with suspicion among the political-bureaucratic establishment, even when they claim to espouse it. The reason is mainly that organized interests succeed at capturing the government and denying the right of ordinary citizens to import what they want if they are offered terms better than those of domestic producers. The main ideology supporting protectionism seems to be nationalism and the espousal of state power.

New Business Interests

Fortunately, a certain level of free trade tends to generate special interests that support it and thus counterbalance the interests pushing for protectionism. American farmers who have benefited from increased exports to Canada and Mexico under NAFTA are worried about the agreement's survival. Canadian piglets are imported to America, fattened up on farms in Iowa, Minnesota, and Illinois, and sometimes reexported in the form of pork cutlets—another example of integrated supply chains, which are also characteristic in the beef trade.[10] The integration of supply chains across the Canadian and Mexican borders means that many American firms now buy many inputs from the other NAFTA countries. Large retailers that import inexpensive goods from China also oppose trade restrictions. Whether the benefits of these international supply chains will successfully counter businesses' natural tendency to conspire against consumers by means of protectionist demands, only time will tell.

ESSAY 7: FREE TRADE AGREEMENTS AND NAFTA

Free trade agreements (FTAs) are treaties between governments in which they agree to reciprocally reduce tariffs or nontariff barriers to trade. Some 400 FTAs exist in the world. The US government is party to 14, including a treaty with Israel (1985) and a major one with Canada and Mexico, the North American Free Trade Agreement (NAFTA), which came into force on January 1, 1994.[11] The other FTAs involving the United States are smaller, and many are merely bilateral agreements that came in force in the new millennium—they include agreements with Jordan, Singapore, Australia, Morocco, South Korea, several Central American and South American countries, and a few others.[12] FTAs approved by the World Trade Organization (WTO) set up preferential tariffs that don't trigger the Most-Favored Nation requirement (whereby a tariff reduction in favor of one country must be made available to all 164 WTO member countries). According to a government estimate, 47 percent of American exports of goods went to trade-agreement partners in 2015.[13]

FTAs have advantages and disadvantages. They are advantageous when they expand the scope of the WTO's trade liberalization rules and promote more trade along the lines of comparative advantage. They can have drawbacks in terms of resource allocation when they create trade diversion—that is, when trade agreements with certain countries dampen trade flows with other countries that have a stronger comparative advantage—in other words, when their discriminatory provisions generate artificial comparative advantages. Another way in which FTAs can generate more costs than benefits is if they incorporate labor or environmental standards that, in fact, limit trade by preventing producers in poor countries from competing with rich-country producers.

As envisioned, NAFTA has presided over a large reduction in trade barriers, to the point where, with a few exceptions, no tariffs now hamper trade between the three countries. Since Mexican tariffs were much higher than American (and Canadian) tariffs, the tariff reduction has been much more beneficial to American exporters than to Mexican exporters. NAFTA also addressed some nontariff barriers to trade in services and to foreign investment.

If NAFTA were abolished now and if both the US and Mexican governments continued to abide by current WTO rules, the average tariff applied to Mexican imports into the United States would be 3.7 percent, and the average tariff applied to American exports to Mexico would increase to 7.4 percent, as shown in figure 7.1. Moreover, because Mexico is a developing country, WTO rules would allow its government to raise its applied tariffs up to a higher "bound rate" of 35 percent on average (as opposed to 7.4 percent). American agricultural exports are among those that would be hit especially hard.

In the same way, other FTAs in which the United States participates have generally reduced foreign tariffs more than American tariffs—simply because the latter were already much lower.[14]

NAFTA has led to a tight integration of supply chains in North America, a large increase in trade, and numerous benefits to consumers. According to some estimates, goods imported from Canada contain 25 percent US inputs, and goods imported from Mexico contain 40 percent US inputs.[15]

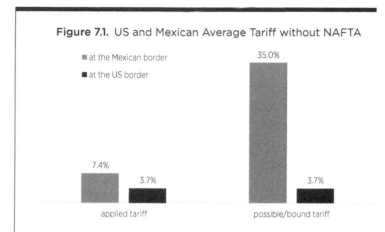

Figure 7.1. US and Mexican Average Tariff without NAFTA

■ at the Mexican border
■ at the US border

applied tariff — 7.4%, 3.7%

possible/bound tariff — 35.0%, 3.7%

Source: Federal Reserve Bank of New York, "U.S. Exporters Could Face High Tariffs Without NAFTA," *Liberty Street Economics*, April 17, 2017.

Mathematical models generally show that NAFTA has only a small positive impact on the American economy.[16] This result is not surprising, given that NAFTA trade remains small compared to the size of the US economy (see figure 7.2).[17] The Congressional Research Service explains, "The overall economic impact of NAFTA is difficult to measure since trade and investment trends are influenced by numerous other economic variables, such as economic growth, inflation, and currency fluctuations."[18] Moreover, the dynamic effects of free trade on economic growth are underestimated, if only because they are more difficult to estimate.

NAFTA has increased trade. Figure 7.2 shows the evolution of American merchandise imports from the other two NAFTA countries (the darker lines) and American merchandise exports to these two countries (the lighter lines). From 1993 to 2016, the value of merchandise imports from and exports to NAFTA countries (top panel) have been multiplied by 2.8 and 2.5, respectively—a faster growth than global US merchandise imports and exports.

NAFTA trade (imports plus exports) now represents about one-third of total US trade in goods and services, about double the share of the trade with China.

Comparing NAFTA trade with US GDP helps give some perspective. In the lower panel of figure 7.2, we see that both imports and exports have increased, from 2.2 percent and 2.1 percent of GDP, respectively, to 3.1 percent and 2.7 percent. The increase in NAFTA trade is certainly important but is not suggestive of large trade diversion—especially since NAFTA covers a contiguous region. Moreover, research suggests that "U.S.-Mexico trade under NAFTA has been trade creating rather than trade diverting."[19]

Figure 7.2. Merchandise Trade of the United States with NAFTA Countries, 1993–2016

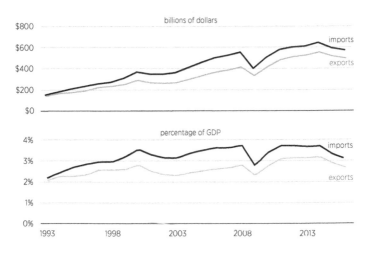

Sources: United States International Trade Commission, "U.S. General Imports, Interactive Tariff and Trade DataWeb," accessed July 18, 2017, http://dataweb.usitc.gov; Bureau of Economic Analysis, table 1.1.5, "Gross Domestic Product," June 29, 2017.

The merchandise deficit (negative balance on goods) within NAFTA is shown by the gap between the two lines in figure 7.2. Although the deficit increased up to the Great Recession in 2008–2009, the recession reduced it, illustrating again that a trade deficit is not a bad thing per se: a deficit means that a country is getting more from its exports. The merchandise deficit with NAFTA countries seems to have plateaued since just after that recession. Moreover, about a third of it is canceled by the surplus in services.[20] Finally, there might not be any merchandise deficit with other NAFTA countries if it were not for imports of petroleum and petroleum products from Canada and Mexico.[21]

In terms of comparative advantage, many of the major US imports from NAFTA countries are also major US exports—for example, oil and gas, motor vehicles and parts, and computer equipment—showing the continental integration of supply chains. The United States seems to have a general comparative advantage in semiconductors (exported mainly to Mexico) and in agricultural and construction machinery (exported mainly to Canada). Nonferrous metals are the main import from Canada; audio and video equipment are the main imports from Mexico.[22]

American consumers benefit from the lower prices of all that is imported from Canada and Mexico, either as inputs or as finished goods. NAFTA could obviously be improved, but it would be by making it more conducive to free trade, not less.

CHAPTER 8

Objection: Free Trade Is Not Fair

It should be fairly obvious by now that the common objections to free trade are without economic foundations. They ultimately rest on a nationalist and interventionist ideology that is inconsistent not only with sound economics but also, as we will see now, with the traditional and very American value of individual liberty. Another objection remains to be confronted: trade is not fair. Addressing (briefly) the notion of fairness will push us into the domain of normative values—what economists also call *value judgments*. Economists, or anybody for that matter, cannot avoid value judgments when they recommend or evaluate public policy, but these judgments must be explicitly recognized and submitted to analysis.

Moral Excuses

The moral concern for fairness is often, if not usually, an excuse. What is blamed as unfair trade is any situation in which one's price is undercut by one's foreign competitor. The outcompeted producer is the one that makes the complaint. Neither consumers nor the most efficient competitors generally call free trade unfair.

Typically, a producer's "unfair" advantage simply derives from comparative advantage. Sometimes comparative advantage is man-made or "artificial," which does not make it less of an actual comparative advantage.[1] Government subsidies are a sort of artificial comparative advantage; there are good reasons to oppose subsidies, but these do not constitute an argument against free trade. Foreign subsidies are not deemed unfair by the consumers (or businesses) who benefit from lower prices. One wonders why people who appreciate subsidies from their own government would reject them when they come from foreign taxpayers. Why should American consumers of subsidized Chinese solar panels find those subsidies unfair? Domestic producers of solar panels, however, use fairness as an excuse for demanding tariffs.[2] Clearly, in this case, fairness is an excuse to defend a material interest. The best solution to the distortions created by government subsidies or other protectionist measures is still to let free trade be free.

The fear that domestic firms will be outcompeted by subsidized foreign producers is not a sufficient argument for a government to prevent its own citizens from making their own import deals. Whatever harm is thereby caused domestically, such as loss of jobs, is no different from damage caused by everyday economic competition, which requires producers to respond to changes in consumer demand and technological innovation. Moreover, the fear of outcompetition is probably exaggerated. State-owned and heavily subsidized companies are typically inefficient, and their handicap rarely diminishes with time. Free and competitive businesses are often able to sustain competition from state corporations for long periods of time. Moreover, it is likely that foreign taxpayers will at some point tire of sending subsidies abroad.

Another protectionist excuse is that free trade leads to the exploitation of poor foreign workers—the so-called *sweatshop argument*.[3] This argument neglects several facts. At least in relatively free labor markets, these workers are poor because their productivity is low. (In unfree countries, they may be exploited by the rulers of their own countries.) Those who choose to work in the export sector do so voluntarily, because working conditions elsewhere in their country are worse. A trade ban or restriction would harm these poor workers by removing the best (or least bad) alternative they have. Marxist economist Joan Robinson realized that "as we see nowadays in South-East Asia or the Caribbean, the misery of being exploited by capitalists is nothing compared to the misery of not being exploited at all."[4] People who agitate for impeding trade with poor countries are typically special-interest groups of rich capitalists and workers threatened by competition from poor workers in these countries.

The fairness argument against free trade often amounts to arguing that, in fact, free competition is impossible against lower-cost producers. From this perspective, competition requires an equal playing field, and foreign cost advantages must be compensated by tariffs at home. Any lower-cost foreign producer must be guilty of "dumping." This old argument was used by early 20th century American protectionists. The Republican Party (which was then more protectionist than the Democratic Party) defended "the true principle of protection," which required a fair equalization of the cost of production across countries. Economist Frank Taussig provided a definitive counterargument:

Anything in the world can be made within a country if the producer is assured of "cost of production together with reasonable profits." . . . Very good pineapples can be grown in Maine, if only a duty be imposed sufficient to equalize the cost of production between the growers in Maine and those in more favored climes. . . . Consistently and thoroughly applied, the "true principle" means that duties shall be high enough to cause anything and everything to be made within the country and international trade to cease.[5]

The Morality of Free Trade

Aside from material interests masquerading as ethics, is there a moral case for fairness in trade? This short book cannot review all moral arguments about free trade,[6] but will instead reflect on the simple ethical principles that seem to flow from the methodology of economics. From this perspective, two points can be safely made.

First, instead of confining free trade to fair trade—instead of defining freedom in terms of fairness and requiring philosophical agreement about what is fair—it seems better to define fairness in terms of liberty. Trade is fair if it is entered into freely by two parties. As philosopher Robert Nozick has argued, socialism needs to "forbid capitalist acts between consenting adults."[7] Free trade is made of capitalist acts between consenting adults. The extreme case of trade in stolen goods can be treated as an exception, not because trade is not fair, but because the goods traded have been obtained unjustly. Another extreme case may be trade with a slave master who offers goods produced by his slaves. At any rate, except for extreme cases, one can argue for the presumption that fairness is liberty and that free trade is fair by definition.

An illustration that free trade is an essential part of the difference between a free and an unfree society was given by George Fitzhugh, a 19th-century defender of slavery, who argued consistently against both liberty and free trade. "Admit liberty to be a good," he wrote, "and you leave no room to argue that free trade is an evil—because liberty is free trade."[8]

Second, if there is a fairness argument to be made in matters of trade, it is that every human being should be treated equally in a formal sense. Protectionism can be in the interest of most people in a large country if—and only if—their government is able to change the terms of trade in their favor. As mentioned previously, this is the only serious argument against free trade—that a large country can manipulate the terms of trade in its favor with optimal tariffs. Even in that case, protectionism remains morally unacceptable in light of the usual methodology of economics and the foundations of a free society. It should be taken for granted, as proposed by the individualist methodology of economics, that all human beings have the same moral weight—whether they are nationals or foreigners, wherever they have been born. The Manchester (classical) liberals of the 19th century, who promoted free trade and the abolition of the Corn Laws, understood that well. John Hicks, winner of the 1972 Nobel Prize in economics, wrote,

> The Manchester Liberals believed in Free Trade not only on the ground of Fairness among Englishmen, but also on the ground of Fairness between Englishmen and foreigners. The State, so they held, ought not to discriminate among its own citizens; also it ought not to discriminate between its own citizens and others.[9]

From this moral point of view, a national government, especially the government of a large and powerful country, should not treat foreigners as second-rate subjects of its empire. A different but related point is that F. A. Hayek's ideal of the "Great Society"—a rule-based order meant to protect the pursuit of individuals' goals—is incompatible with protectionism, which is arguably a residual of our forebears' tribal fear of strangers.[10]

Another claim against free trade is that it entails a loss of national sovereignty. To the extent that this argument means the power of a national state over its citizens is diminished, it is an argument in favor of free trade, not against it. Free trade moves the sovereignty from the national level to the individual level. If national sovereignty means instead the capacity of the US government to protect individual liberty, then it cannot be invoked against citizens who want to import goods and services from beyond the national borders.

As a matter of fact, there is no "level playing field" in the economy, whether domestic or international, and it cannot be created without social-engineering powers that are inimical to a free society. The most we can hope for is legal rules guaranteeing an equal formal liberty to everybody. Free trade does not mean fair trade, except if "fair" is defined as "free."

To summarize, free trade *is* fair trade. The fair trade argument is usually an excuse for special interests or for state power. What is fair is to let each individual or private entity reach its own bargains. Even if domestic protectionism can favor some people in their own countries at the cost of harming foreigners, and especially poorer foreigners, it does not seem morally acceptable. And remember that protectionism essentially means a government's control over what its own citizens or subjects may import, and under what conditions.

ESSAY 8: AMERICAN CONSUMERS BENEFIT FROM TRADE WITH CHINA

For Americans, China is the third largest export market (after Canada and Mexico) and the largest foreign supplier of goods. Total trade with China (exports of goods and services plus imports of goods and services) is lower than with NAFTA (Canada and Mexico conjoined), mainly because more than twice the value of American exports goes to NAFTA than to China. Imports from China are 18 percent of total American imports, while exports to China are 8 percent of total American exports.

The $310 billion trade deficit with China, which accounts for 61 percent of the total US trade deficit ($505 billion), has been much demonized, but we saw there is no a priori reason to be concerned—much less obsessed—with a trade deficit.[11] What is important is how imports from China benefit American consumers.

Americans buy from China mainly machinery (including electronic devices assembled there but conceived and engineered in the United States), furniture, toys and sports equipment, and clothing and shoes (mainly shoes). But this represents only a small part of what Americans consume. This is because American consumers, similarly to consumers in other advanced economies, buy more services than goods—about two-thirds of what American consumers buy are services, such as health, housing, recreation, education, and financial services, which are typically not traded internationally. So it is not surprising to find that nearly 90 percent of what American consumers buy has been made in America, and only 2.7 percent is "made in China."

Figure 8.1 displays this 2.7 percent share that goods marked "made in China" occupy in personal consumption expenditures in the United States. The smallest circle illustrates the share of these made-in-China goods that is actually paid to Chinese exporters—1.2 percent—because 55 percent of the final cost to the consumer of imported Chinese goods represents services produced in the United States to transport, sell, and market these goods inside the country. In other words, the American content of goods "made in China" is about 55 percent. Hence, only 1.2 percent of what American consumers spend goes toward what is made by Chinese residents.

The small proportion (barely more than 1 percent) of their budgets that American consumers spend on goods actually made in China does not mean that these are not

Figure 8.1. Imports from China in US Consumption Expenditures, 2010

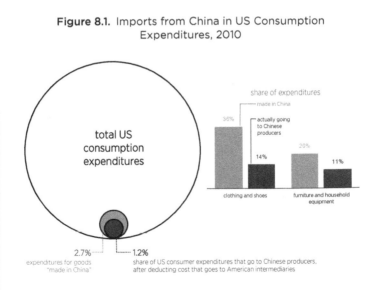

Source: Galina Hale and Bart Hobijn, "The U.S. Content of 'Made in China,'" FRBSF Economic Letter, Federal Reserve Bank of San Francisco, August 8, 2011.

important. Any purchase that consumers make serves to maximize their net benefits. Consumers have more to spend on whatever they want if the prices of certain goods decrease, other things being equal. The right-hand charts in figure 8.1 show that consumers import from China (via intermediaries such as stores) a significant fraction of what they consume in the categories "furniture and household equipment" and "clothing and shoes." Respectively one-fifth and more than one-third of these are labeled "made in China." Deducting the part of the cost of these imports that actually goes to American intermediaries, we find that consumers devote more than one-tenth of their budgets for these goods to things produced by residents of China.[12]

It is interesting to note that the industries where American consumers spend the largest proportion of their budgets on Chinese imports have benefited from large price drops since 2001 (the year at the end of which China joined the WTO). While the general consumer price index (CPI) increased by 35.5 percent between 2001 and 2016, the CPI component "apparel" (clothing and shoes) dropped by 1.0 percent, the component "furniture and bedding" dropped by 15.2 percent, and the component "appliances" dropped by 19.1 percent.[13] Since the prices of these goods decreased while general inflation was positive, their real prices dropped even more.

Any family knows that the prices of shoes, furniture, and appliances have decreased for a given quality and, often, for a better quality. Imports from China are not the only factor that played a role (prices started declining in the mid- or late-1990s), but they certainly contributed, as did imports from other poor countries. American consumers have benefited—and especially the poorer ones, as argued in essay 5.

Conclusion

This book has considered a number of common objections to free trade and found them wanting. The efficiency of free trade is not hampered by lower wages in foreign countries. Free trade has greater benefits than costs for the individuals who compose a country—and a country is nothing but the individuals who live there. Trade deficits do not matter as such, and retaliation against protectionist measures adopted by other countries is nearly always a bad move. To say that the United States is losing its factories is misleading. What has been happening for several decades, in the United States as in other advanced economies, is that firms are specializing in high-end manufacturing and using more productive but less numerous workers, all while increasing or maintaining total manufacturing production. Technological change plays a larger role than trade in the current disruption of manufacturing. Free trade generally does not push down real wages; on the contrary, it boosts productivity and economic growth and thus increases overall incomes. Free trade is the embodiment of any acceptable ideal of fairness.

In the process of responding to common objections, this book has provided a positive defense of free trade in light of economic analysis. Most people benefit from international trade, in the sense that its total benefits are higher than its total costs. Just as technological progress and competition in general do, international trade can create short-run disruptions and harm some individuals, but these economic losses will be more than compensated for by the gains of the vast majority of people. One could object to the losses if they were coercively imposed, but they are merely the consequences of other people exercising their equal liberty to buy goods and services where they want. No producer, even a domestic one, should have the right to force somebody to buy from him or pay him a tax if he buys from somebody else.

Even if a large country's protectionist measures could turn the terms of trade in its favor, there is no justification for doing so, for a number of reasons. First, free trade still produces net benefits at the world level. Second, protectionist measures can lead to retaliation and worldwide trade restrictions, which harm all countries. Third, free trade has dynamic benefits in the sense of promoting economic growth. Fourth, the politics of protectionism necessarily favor powerful interest groups instead of maximizing economic opportunities for most people. Protectionism is subject to the usual inefficiencies of political and bureaucratic processes. Market failures are not necessarily worse than political failures—that is, the failures of politicians and bureaucrats to solve problems while respecting individual preferences.

The more free trade in the world, the better, but the minimum requirement and the most practical demand to make is that one's own government not prohibit one from importing freely. Protectionism mainly harms people in the very countries whose governments impose it. A practical goal is to free one's own country before trying to persuade foreign protectionist governments to abolish the restraints on their citizens. A protectionist foreign government will not in any case be able to push its producers to export while its consumers import nothing, for the foreign currency gained through exports must be spent on foreign goods or foreign investment, or else sold on financial markets (and then the protectionist country's currency will appreciate and reestablish the balance-of-payment equilibrium). When a national government promotes exports, it *ipso facto* encourages imports (or the outflow of capital). So we should concentrate on the liberty to import; our capacity to export, which typically lies in the hands of foreign governments, will likely take care of itself.

The rules of the WTO and those of specific free trade agreements like NAFTA are useful as ways to tie the hands of national governments and avoid trade wars, which benefit no one. Ulysses asked to be tied to his ship's mast in order to resist the temptation of the sirens. The WTO and free trade agreements can be seen as means to similarly render a national government incapable of yielding to the appeal of domestic rent-seekers and the sirens of protectionism. International trade agreements and institutions are useful to the extent that they protect free trade—as opposed to impeding it with stifling harmonization.

Perhaps, with some optimism, we may hope that, in the future, an understanding of the economics of trade will persuade citizens to demand that their own governments recognize their liberty to import. We may also hope that people on the Left or on the Right will realize that the only way to protect oneself against a government one does not like is to reduce government power in general, and that free trade is one important means of reducing government power.

British economist Thomas Farrer wrote, "When I was asked in 1880 by the president of the Cobden Club to write something in defense of Free Trade, it seemed to me—recollecting as I did the instruction in politics which I had received from the Corn Law Controversy—as if I had been asked to prove Euclid."[1] The "Corn Law Controversy" to which he refers ended with the repeal of the Corn Laws by the British government in 1846, after the common people had realized that the limitation of grain imports increased the price of bread. (Businessman Richard Cobden was a leader of the movement.) But free trade is arguably a bit more complicated than Farrer's statement suggests. One can find some theoretical cases in which most residents of a country will be benefited by their own government's protectionist measures. But these cases are rare and they can never make the whole world better off. In practice, protectionism amounts to a coercive redistribution of income from some individuals to other individuals—generally to well-organized and well-connected special interests—mainly within the protectionist country itself. So Farrer was broadly right, as most students of economics discover when they learn the theory of international trade.

Ultimately, the benefits of free international trade simply instantiate the general benefits of exchange, and parallel the benefits of domestic trade. After his masterful review of the intellectual history of free trade, Douglas Irwin concludes that "the broad presumption behind free trade has not been substantially undercut, but has remained intact."[2] Protectionism is not so much directed against foreigners as against nationals who are prevented from importing the goods and services that they want on the best terms they can find. Supporting free markets and opposing international free trade is not a coherent position. It is in the interest of the vast majority of Americans for the country to move closer to free trade and farther away from protectionism. More free trade is needed, not less.

Notes

Introduction

1. Douglas A. Irwin, *Against the Tide: An Intellectual History of Free Trade* (Princeton, NJ: Princeton University Press, 1996), chapter 2.

2. Paul R. Krugman, Maurice Obstfeld, and Marc Melitz, *International Trade: Theory and Policy*, 10th ed. (Boston: Addison-Wesley, 2015).

3. Krugman, Obstfeld, and Melitz, *International Trade*, 240.

4. Daniel B. Klein, William L. Davis, and David Hedengren, "Economics Professors' Voting, Policy Views, Favorite Economists, and Frequent Lack of Consensus," *Econ Journal Watch* 10, no. 1 (January 2013): 116–25.

5. For a discussion focusing on the Trans-Pacific Partnership, see Pierre Lemieux, "Free Trade and TPP," *Library of Economics and Liberty*, February 1, 2016.

6. Douglas A. Irwin, *Free Trade under Fire*, 4th ed. (Princeton, NJ: Princeton University Press, 2015), 22–23. (Note that the two lines on p. 23 have been mistakenly inverted.) Will Martin and Aaditya Mattoo, *Unfinished Business? The WTO's Doha Agenda* (Washington, DC: International Bank for Reconstruction and Development/World Bank, 2011), 6, 48, 49, 63, and 65.

7. United States International Trade Commission, *Harmonized Tariff Schedule of the United States (2017)—Revision 1*, July 2017.

8. "The President-Elect's Perilous Trade Policy," *Economist*, January 7, 2017.

9. United States Department of Agriculture, Sugar and Sweeteners Yearbook Tables, table 3b and table 4 (update of August 1, 2017), at https://www.ers.usda.gov/data-products/sugar-and-sweeteners-yearbook-tables/ (accessed August 7, 2017) and https://hts.usitc.gov/current (accessed August 15, 2017).

10. Export taxes or duties on exports are prohibited by the Constitution, but other restrictions are possible, as illustrated by the oil export restrictions that were only recently abolished. On the constitutional question, see Douglas A. Irwin, *Clashing over Commerce: A History of Trade Policy* (Chicago: University of Chicago Press, 2017), 62–64. In general, import restrictions have been the main foreign-trade impediment imposed on Americans. This is another reason to focus on free trade as the freedom to import. I reviewed Irwin's book in "Patriotism as Stealing from Each Other," *Regulation* 40, no. 4 (Winter 2017/18): 64–69.

1. Objection: Americans Cannot Compete against Low-Cost Foreign Producers

1. Benjamin Powell, *Out of Poverty: Sweatshops in the Global Economy* (New York: Cambridge University Press, 2014), 57.

2. Gary Clyde Hufbauer, Cathleen Cimino, and Tyler Moran, "NAFTA at 20: Misleading Charges and Positive Achievements" (Number PB14-13, Peterson Institute for International Economics, Washington, DC, May 2014), 8.

3. *View of Real Grievances, with Remedies Proposed for Redressing Them, Humbly Submitted to the Consideration of the Legislature* (London, 1772), 281. (Published anonymously, the book is attributed to John Powell.) The passage is also quoted in Irwin, *Against the Tide*, 154.

4. Adam Smith, *An Inquiry into the Nature and Causes of the Wealth of Nations*, ed. Edwin Cannan (London: Methuen, 1904 [1776]).

5. David Ricardo, *On the Principles of Political Economy*, 3rd ed. (London: J. M. Dent, 1911 [1817, 1821]), 81–84. The theory of comparative advantage was intuited (or perhaps even codiscovered) by two other economists of the same period, James Mill and Robert Torrens. On this historical controversy, see Irwin, *Against the Tide*, 89–91.

6. Of course, if his business is small, Mark may prefer to purchase an "accounting robot"—automated accounting software—from another party.

7. A more formal proof of the theory of comparative advantage can be found in any good economics textbook on macroeconomics or international trade. See also Lauren F. Landsburg, "Comparative Advantage," *Library of Economics and Liberty*, accessed January 22, 2017. For a numerical example, see Donald J. Boudreaux, "Comparative Advantage," in *The Concise Encyclopedia of Economics*, ed. David R. Henderson, 2nd ed. (Indianapolis: Library of Economics and Liberty, 2008).

8. Paul R. Krugman, "What Should Trade Negotiators Negotiate About?," *Journal of Economic Literature* 35, no. 1 (March 1997): 115.

9. For a more elaborate argument, see Donald J. Boudreaux, "Does Increased International Mobility of Factors of Production Weaken the Case for Free Trade?," *Cato Journal* 23, no. 3 (2004): 373–79.

10. See Council of Economic Advisers, *Economic Report of the President*, February 2005, p. 175.

11. Krugman, Obstfeld, and Melitz, *International Trade*, 47.

12. Béla Balassa, "An Empirical Demonstration of Classical Comparative Cost Theory," *Review of Economics and Statistics* 45, no. 3 (1963): 231–38.

13. On the importance of legal institutions favorable to private property rights, see Nita Ghei, "Institutional Arrangements, Property Rights, and the Endogenity of Comparative Advantage," *Transnational Law and Contemporary Problems* 18 (Summer 2009).

14. Hufbauer, Cimino, and Moran, "NAFTA at 20," 8. These rates are reported for 2014.

15. The main American exports to and imports from Mexico are listed in the Mexico sheet of the Office of the United States Trade Representative, accessed August 16, 2017, https://ustr.gov/countries-regions/americas /mexico.

16. International Monetary Fund, World Bank, and World Trade Organization, "Making Trade an Engine of Growth for All: The Case for Trade and for Policies to Facilitate Adjustment," April 10, 2017, p. 48.

17. Scott C. Bradford, Paul L. E. Grieco, and Gary Clyde Hufbauer, "The Payoff to America from Global Integration," in *The United States and the World Economy*, ed. C. Fred Bergsten (Washington, DC: Institute for International Economics, 2005).

18. Gary Clyde Hufbauer and Zhiyao Lu, "The Payoff to America from Globalization: A Fresh Look with a Focus on Costs to Workers" (Policy Brief 17-16, Peterson Institute for International Economics, Washington, DC, May 2017), especially pp. 6, 7, 21, and 23.

19. Eric Nelson, "Global Supply Chains Explained . . . in One Graphic," US Chamber of Commerce, May 2, 2016.

20. Bureau of Economic Analysis, table 1.2, "U.S. International Transactions," lines 10 and 20 for 2016, released June 20, 2017. For other facts reported in this essay, see also Council of Economic Advisers, *The Economic Benefits of U.S. Trade*, May 2015.

21. Bureau of Economic Analysis, "U.S. International Economic Accounts: Concepts and Methods," June 2014. US Census Bureau and Bureau of Economic Analysis, *U.S. International Trade in Goods and Services*, June 2017. Council of Economic Advisers, *Economic Report of the President*, 178.

22. Bob Davis, "How a U.S. Textile Maker Came to Embrace Free Trade," *Wall Street Journal*, May 4, 2015.

2. Objection: Free Trade Harms the United States

1. James Mill, *Elements of Political Economy* (London: Baldwin, Cradock, and Joy, 1821), 89; also quoted in Irwin, *Against the Tide*, 91. Emphasis in original.

2. French economist Frédéric Bastiat gives a similar example in *Oeuvres complètes de Frédéric Bastiat*, vol. 4, *Sophismes économiques* (Paris: Guillaumin et Cie, 1863), translated by Arthur Goddard as *Economic Sophisms* (Irvington-on-Hudson, NY: Foundation for Economic Education, 1996).

3. Jagdish Bhagwati, introduction to *Going Alone: The Case for Relaxed Reciprocity in Freeing Trade*, ed. Jagdish Bhagwati (Cambridge, MA: MIT Press, 2002), 6.

4. Economists often make this argument; for example, "Only individuals trade, and not nation states, and the well-being of individuals, not of any organic entity, should be the rationale of trade policy." Charles K. Rowley, Willem Thorbecke, and Richard E. Wagner, *Trade Protection in the United States* (Aldershot, UK: Edward Elgar, 1995), 239.

5. Economics textbooks give an algebraic or graphical proof of this proposition. See, for example, Krugman, Obstfeld, and Melitz, *International Trade*, 212–28. What follows is an attempt to render the essential argument in plain English.

6. The optimal tariff argument is often called the *terms-of-trade* argument.

7. World Trade Organization, *World Trade Statistical Review: 2016*, 95, table A7.

8. "Gross Domestic Product 2015," World Development Indicators database, World Bank, accessed January 11, 2017.

9. Executive Office of the President, *The Economic Benefit of U.S. Trade*, May 2015, 13.

10. "President-Elect's Perilous Trade Policy," *Economist*.

11. On social organicism and methodological individualism, see Friedrich A. Hayek, *The Counter-Revolution of Science: Studies on the Abuse of Reason* (Indianapolis: Liberty Fund, 1979 [1952]), especially chapters 4 and 6; and Friedrich A. Hayek, *Law, Legislation and Liberty*, vol. 1, *Rules and Order* (Chicago: University of Chicago Press, 1973), especially chapter 2.

12. Wilbur Ross, "Mr. Trump Makes Some Good Points on Trade," *Wall Street Journal*, August 14, 2016.

13. See, for example, Tyler Cowen and Alex Tabarrok, *Modern Principles: Macroeconomics* (New York: Worth Publishers, 2010), 78—but any good textbook will do.

14. For further discussion and references, see Pierre Lemieux, "What You Always Wanted to Know about GDP but Were Afraid to Ask," *Regulation* 39, no. 4 (2016–2017): 64–69; Pierre Lemieux, "Are Imports a Drag on the Economy?," *Regulation* 38, no. 3 (2015): 6–8.

Notes

3. Objection: The Trade Deficit Is Bad

1. See figure 3.1 in essay 3 and its sources. See also Jeffrey G. Williamson, *American Growth and the Balance of Payments, 1820–1913: A Study of the Long Swing* (Chapel Hill, NC: University of North Carolina Press, 1964); and Donald J. Boudreaux, "If Trade Surpluses Are So Great, the 1930s Should Have Been a Booming Decade," *Cafe Hayek*, December 21, 2006.

2. See table 3.1 in essay 3.

3. Bureau of Economic Analysis, US International Investment Position Tables, table 1.2, released June 28, 2017, https://www.bea.gov/scb/pdf/2017/07 percent 20July/0717_international_investment_position_tables.pdf. See also Daniel Griswold, *Mad about Trade: Why Main Street America Should Embrace Globalization* (Washington, DC: Cato Institute, 2009), 83.

4. See Arnold Kling, "International Trade," in *The Concise Encyclopedia of Economics*, ed. David R. Henderson, 2nd ed. (Indianapolis: Library of Economics and Liberty, 2008).

5. "How to Improve NAFTA," *Economist*, August 19, 2017.

6. United States Government Accountability Office, *Financial Audit: Bureau of the Fiscal Service's Fiscal Years 2016 and 2015 Schedules of Federal Debt* (GAO-17-104, Government Accountability Office, Washington, DC, November 2016), 2 and 17 for the data on the debt held by the public and the proportion held outside the United States.

7. See also Griswold, *Mad about Trade*, chapter 5.

8. Krugman, "What Should Trade Negotiators Negotiate About?," 113.

9. Joan Robinson, *Essays in the Theory of Employment* (Oxford: Basil Blackwell, 1947), 158.

10. See also Donald J. Boudreaux, "Do Subsidies Justify Retaliatory Protectionism?," *Economic Affairs* 31, no. 3 (2011), 4–6.

11. "America Lifts Its Ban on Oil Exports," *Economist*, December 18, 2015; Alison Sider, "U.S. Exports First Freely Traded Oil in 40 Years," *Wall Street Journal*, January 13, 2016.

12. As I note in an earlier book, for several decades ending in the early 19th century, the British government banned the export of some industrial machinery—as well as the emigration of skilled workers—in order to prevent foreign textile manufacturers from competing with British manufacturers. Pierre Lemieux, *Who Needs Jobs? Spreading Poverty or Increasing Welfare* (New York: Macmillan, 2014), 91. See also David J. Jeremy, "Damming the Flood: British Government Efforts to Check the Outflow of Technicians and Machinery," *Business History Review* 51, no. 1 (Spring 1977), 1–34.

13. Robert E. Lipsey, "U.S. Foreign Trade and the Balance of Payments, 1800–1913" (NBER Working Paper No. 4710, National Bureau of Economic Research, Cambridge, MA, April 1994), 10–11.

14. In *Mad about Trade*, Daniel Griswold finds that, from the early 1980s to 2008, there has been an *inverse* relationship between the *rate of change* in the trade deficit and in the rate of unemployment (see pp. 80–82).

4. Objection: The United States Is Losing Its Factories

1. Bureau of Economic Analysis, table 2.1, "U.S. International Trade in Goods and Services," June 20, 2017.

2. Bureau of Labor Statistics, "All Employees: Manufacturing" (CEU3000000001), data retrieved from FRED Economic Data, Federal Reserve Bank of St. Louis, July 27, 2017, https://fred.stlouisfed.org/series/CEU3000000001.

3. US Census Bureau, "Industry Snapshot: Manufacturing," accessed August 17, 2017, http://thedataweb.rm.census.gov/TheDataWeb_HotReport2/econsnapshot/2012/snapshot.hrml?NAICS=31-33.

4. Bureau of Labor Statistics, "Percent of Employment in Manufacturing in Different Countries (Discontinued)," data retrieved from FRED Economic Data, Federal Reserve Bank of St. Louis, accessed March 5, 2017, https://fred.stlouisfed.org/graph/?graph_id=366462&rn=4989. Economists Robert Rowthorn and Ramana Ramaswamy report that the share of manufacturing employment in industrial countries declined from 28 percent to 18 percent between 1970 and 1994; see their article "Growth, Trade, and Deindustrialization" (IMF Working Paper WP/98/60, International Monetary Fund, Washington, DC, March 1999), 18. See also "Politicians Cannot Bring Back Old-Fashioned Factory Jobs," *Economist*, January 14, 2017.

5. David H. Autor and Anna Salomons, "Does Productivity Growth Threaten Employment?" (paper presented at the European Central Bank Forum on Central Banking, June 27, 2017), notably pp. 25, 26, and 52.

6. Bureau of Labor Statistics, "Civilian Employment Level" (LNU02000000) and "All Employees: Manufacturing" (CEU3000000001), data retrieved from FRED Economic Data, Federal Reserve Bank of St. Louis, July 27, 2017, https://fred.stlouisfed.org/series/LNU02000000 and https://fred.stlouisfed.org/series/CEU3000000001. Another measure, which has nonfarm labor (instead of civilian labor force) in the denominator, is slightly higher and shows a peak of 38 percent in 1943: see Bureau of Labor Statistics, "All Employees: Total Nonfarm Payrolls" (PAYEMS), data retrieved from FRED Economic Data, Federal Reserve Bank of St. Louis, August 17, 2017, https://fred.stlouisfed.org/series/PAYEMS.

7. Bureau of Labor Statistics, "All Employees: Manufacturing" (CEU3000000001), data retrieved from FRED Economic Data, Federal Reserve Bank of St. Louis, July 27, 2017, https://fred.stlouisfed.org/series/CEU3000000001.

8. Bureau of Economic Analysis, "Value Added by Industry as a Percentage of Gross Domestic Product," November 3, 2016.

9. Board of Governors of the Federal Reserve System (US), "Industrial Production: Manufacturing (NAICS)" (IPGMFNQ), data retrieved from FRED Economic Data, Federal Reserve Bank of St. Louis, July 14, 2017, https://fred.stlouisfed.org/series/IPGMFNQ.

10. The earliest year available for this data is 1997. For the Real Value Added in Manufacturing, see Bureau of Economic Analysis, "Chain-Type Quantity Indexes for Value Added by Industry," April 21, 2017.

11. On this point, it is worth reading "Politicians Cannot Bring Back Old-Fashioned Factory Jobs," *Economist*.

12. Andrew B. Bernard, Valerie Smeets, and Frederic Warzynski make this point for Denmark. See Bernard, Smeets, and Warzynski, "Rethinking Deindustrialization" (NBER Working Paper No. 22114, National Bureau of Economic Research, Cambridge, MA, March 2016).

13. See "Slicing an Apple," *Economist*, August 10, 2011; "iPadded," *Economist*, January 21, 2012; "Politicians Cannot Bring Back Old-Fashioned Factory Jobs," *Economist*.

14. "Politicians Cannot Bring Back Old-Fashioned Factory Jobs," *Economist*.

15. David Dollar, "Global Economic Forces Conspire to Stymie US Manufacturing," Brookings Institution, December 29, 2016.

16. Bernard, Smeets, and Warzynski, "Rethinking Deindustrialization."

17. Bernard, Smeets, and Warzynski, 16.

18. Autor and Salomons, "Does Productivity Growth Threaten Employment?"

19. See Daniel Griswold, "The Real Story behind the Loss of Steelworker Jobs," *Mad about Trade* (blog), July 5, 2017.

5. Objection: Trade Destroys Jobs

1. Economists use "welfare" as a technical term to label and analyze the "utility" or "satisfaction" of individuals. The concept is entirely different from the political concept of government assistance.

2. See Pierre Lemieux, *Who Needs Jobs?*

3. For estimates of the elasticity of labor supply, see Raj Chetty, "Bounds on Elasticities with Optimization Frictions: A Synthesis of Micro and Macro Evidence on Labor Supply," *Econometrica* 80, no. 3 (May 2012): 969–1018.

4. Casey B. Mulligan, *The Redistribution Recession: How Labor Market Distortions Contracted the Economy* (New York: Oxford University Press, 2012).

5. Gallup, "State of the American Workplace," accessed March 5, 2017.

6. Autor and Salomons, "Does Productivity Growth Threaten Employment?"

7. See David H. Autor, David Dorn, and Gordon H. Hanson, "The China Shock: Learning from Labor Market Adjustment to Large Changes in Trade" (NBER Working Paper No. 21906, National Bureau of Economic Research, Cambridge, MA, January 2016), 28–29; Pierre Lemieux, "Trade and Adjustment Costs," *Regulation* 39, no. 3 (2016): 10–11.

8. Jonathan T. Rothwell, "Cutting the Losses: Reassessing the Costs of Import Competition to Workers and Communities" (George Washington University Institute of Public Policy, Washington, DC, 2017).

9. David H. Autor, David Dorn, and Gordon H. Hanson, "Comment on Jonathan Rothwell's Critique of Autor, Dorn, and Hanson (2013)," March 3, 2017, https://economics.mit.edu/files/12729.

10. Michael J. Hicks and Srikant Devaraj, *The Myth and the Reality of Manufacturing in America* (Muncie, IN: Center for Business and Economic Research, Ball State University, 2015), 6.

11. Charles Roxburgh et al., *Trading Myths: Addressing Misconceptions about Trade, Jobs, and Competitiveness* (McKinsey Global Institute, May 2012).

12. Rowthorn and Ramaswamy, "Growth, Trade, and Deindustrialization."

13. From 1999 to 2011, civilian employment in the United States increased from 133.5 million to 139.9 million. Bureau of Labor Statistics, "Civilian Employment Level" (CE16OV), data retrieved from FRED Economic Data, Federal Reserve Bank of St. Louis, accessed May 19, 2017, https://fred.stlouisfed.org/series/CE16OV.

14. Irwin, *Free Trade under Fire*, 14.

15. See David Autor, "David Autor on Trade, China, and U.S. Labor Markets," interview by Russ Roberts, *EconTalk*, March 14, 2016.

16. Autor, Dorn, and Hanson, "China Shock," 38.

17. Bob Davis, "How a U.S. Textile Maker Came to Embrace Free Trade," *Wall Street Journal*, May 4, 2015.

18. Nassau William Senior, *Three Lectures on the Transmission of the Precious Metals from Country to Country and the Mercantile Theory of Wealth* (London: J. Murray, 1828), 59–60.

19. The evidence is reported in a recent review by the International Monetary Fund, the World Bank, and the World Trade Organization, "Making Trade an Engine of Growth for All."

20. See International Monetary Fund, World Bank, and World Trade Organization, "Making Trade an Engine of Growth for All," 19–20, and the references cited there.

21. Smith, *An Inquiry into the Nature and Causes of the Wealth of Nations*.

22. See the company's *2016 Annual Report*, which emphasizes its commitment to the long run, and states, "We have never declared or paid cash dividends on our common stock" (available at http://phx.corporate-ir.net/phoenix.zhtml?c =97664&p=irol-reportsannual, accessed November 20, 2016).

23. Prabirjit Sarkar, "Trade Openness and Growth: Is There Any Link?," *Journal of Economic Issues* 42, no. 3 (September 2008): 763–85.

24. Sarkar, "Trade Openness and Growth," 772.

25. Andreas Billmeier and Tommaso Nannicini, "Trade Openness and Growth: Pursuing Empirical *Glasnost*" (IMF Working Paper WP/07/156, International Monetary Fund, Washington, DC, June 2007).

26. Romain Wacziarg and Karen Horn Welch, "Trade Liberalization and Growth: New Evidence," *World Bank Economic Review* 22, no. 2 (2008): 187–231.

27. Wacziarg and Horn Welch, "Trade Liberalization and Growth," 212. For further evidence, see, for example, Antoni Estevadeordal and Alan M. Taylor, "Is the Washington Consensus Dead? Growth, Openness, and the Great Liberalization, 1970s–2000s," *Review of Economics and Statistics* 95, no. 5 (December 2013): 1669–90.

28. Lill Andersen and Ronald Babula, "The Link between Openness and Long-Run Economic Growth," *Journal of International Commerce and Economics* (July 2008): 13. See also International Monetary Fund, World Bank, and World Trade Organization, "Making Trade an Engine of Growth for All."

29. Wacziarg and Horn Welsh, "Trade Liberalization and Growth," 209–12.

30. Krugman, Obstfeld, and Melitz, *International Trade*, 282–84. As its name indicates, *import substitution* refers to protectionist measures designed to substitute domestic production for imports.

31. Cary Clyde Hufbauer and Sean Lowry, *US Tire Tariffs: Saving Few Jobs at High Cost*, Peterson Institute for International Economics, April 2012. See also International Monetary Fund, World Bank, and World Trade Organization, "Making Trade an Engine of Growth for All," 21.

32. Wacziarg and Horn Welch, "Trade Liberalization and Growth," 212.

33. This calculation uses Autor, Dorn, and Hanson's figures from "China Shock"; see chapter 5.

34. Bureau of Labor Statistics, table 1, "Private Sector Gross Job Gains and Job Losses, Annual March to March," Annual Business Employment Dynamics Data, accessed November 21, 2017, https://www.bls.gov/web/cewbd/anntab1

_1.txt. Looking instead at the number of Americans who switch jobs during a year (often going from one existing job to another), the numbers are even more impressive, although less representative of the jobs that disappear or are created (thanks to Daniel Griswold for pointing this out): in 2016, there were 60.4 million separations on the American job market and 62.7 million hires; each of these numbers represents more than 40 percent of the number of employed people during that year. See US Bureau of Labor Statistics, "Job Openings, Hires, and Separations Rise, but at a Slower Pace, in 2016," *Monthly Labor Review*, August 2017, 6 and 9.

35. Autor and Salomons, "Does Productivity Growth Threaten Employment?," 6.

36. Jean-Baptiste Say, *Traité d'économie politique* (1803), translated by C. R. Prinsep as *A Treatise on Political Economy* (Philadelphia: Claxton, Remsen & Haffelfinger, 1880). See also "Say's Law: Supply Creates Its Own Demand," *Economist*, August 10, 2017.

37. Pablo D. Fajgelbaum and Amit K. Khandelwal, "Measuring the Unequal Gains from Trade," *Quarterly Journal of Economics* 131, no. 3 (August 2016): 1113–80, table 4. Of course, such model-based counterfactuals should be handled with care.

38. United States International Trade Commission, *Economic Impact of Trade Agreements Implemented under Trade Authorities Procedures, 2016 Report*, June 2016, 23.

6. Objection: Trade Lowers Wages

1. Krugman, Obstfeld, and Melitz, *International Trade*, 39. See also essay 6.

2. See Bertil G. Ohlin, *Interregional and International Trade* (Cambridge, MA: Harvard University Press, 1933); Eli Heckscher, "The Effect of Foreign Trade on the Distribution of Income," in *Readings in the Theory of International Trade*, ed. H. Ellis and L. Metzler (Philadelphia: Blakiston, 1949). Ohlin had been a student of Heckscher, who originally conceived the theory later developed by his student; hence it is attributed to both.

3. There is one theoretical exception to this conclusion, as shown by the Stolper-Samuelson theorem. Wolfgang F. Stolper and Paul A. Samuelson, "Protection and Real Wages," *Review of Economic Studies* 9 (1941): 58–73. See also "An Inconvenient Iota of Truth," *Economist*, August 6, 2016. Stolper and Samuelson demonstrated that in a world with two factors of production—say, capital and labor—wages will fall in real terms when labor is the relatively scarce factor of production, because all prices cannot fall as much as wages. As Stolper and Samuelson themselves pointed out, however, their theorem is valid only in limited circumstances. One crucial limitation is that it does not generalize to the case of more than two factors of production. For example, if there are many types of labor (say, specialized and unspecialized), the theorem

cannot be proved. Because of these limitations, the Stolper-Samuelson theorem remains more a theoretical curiosity than a justification for protectionism.

4. See Donald J. Boudreaux, "Trump on Trade," *Cafe Hayek*, January 17, 2017. The pie analogy that I am using here is not without danger and should be handled carefully: see Pierre Lemieux, "Social Welfare, State Intervention, and Value Judgments," *Independent Review* 11, no 1 (Summer 2006): 19–36.

5. "America's Uncompetitive Markets Harm Its Economy," *Economist*, July 27, 2017.

6. Kathryn G. Marshall, "International Productivity and Factor Price Comparisons," *Journal of International Economics* 87 (2012): 388. The data are nominal wages, which remind us that higher productivity also increases nominal wages if prices are constant. By pushing down the prices of consumption goods, trade further increases the benefits of workers as consumers (as emphasized in the text).

7. "Some college" refers to those who left college before obtaining a bachelor's degree and to those who obtained an associate degree but no bachelor's degree.

8. Bureau of Labor Statistics, "More Education Still Means More Pay in 2014," *Economics Daily*, September 2, 2015.

9. See Autor and Salomons, "Does Productivity Growth Threaten Employment?" The authors' database includes 19 developed countries: the United States and most countries of Western Europe, plus Australia, Japan, and South Korea.

7. The Politics of Trade and a Bit More Economics

1. Mancur Olson, *The Logic of Collective Action: Public Goods and the Theory of Groups* (Cambridge, MA: Harvard University Press, 1965).

2. John C. Beghin and Amani Elobeid, "The Impact of the US Sugar Program Redux," *Applied Economic Perspectives and Policy* 37, no. 1 (2015): 1–33. Krugman, Obstfeld, and Melitz, *International Trade*, 221–23. United States Department of Agriculture, "Sugar and Sweeteners Yearbook Tables," table 3b and table 4. The political contribution figures come from Krugman, Obstfeld, and Melitz, *International Trade*, 223.

3. Frank W. Taussig, *The Tariff History of the United States*, 6th ed. (New York: G. P. Putnam's Sons, 1914), 457.

4. Irwin, *Free Trade under Fire*, 189. On steel and steel protectionism, see also Griswold, "Real Story behind the Loss of Steelworker Jobs"; and Daniel Griswold, "Steeled for Politics," *U.S. News and World Report*, June 26, 2017. On the history of the American steel industry, see Robert P. Rogers, *An Economic History of the American Steel Industry* (London: Routledge, 2009).

5. For a similar analysis of protectionism in the tradition of public choice economics, see Rowley, Thorbecke, and Wagner, *Trade Protection in the United States*.

6. See Friedrich A. Hayek, "The Use of Knowledge in Society," *American Economic Review* 35, no. 4 (1945): 519–30, reproduced in Friedrich A. Hayek, *Individualism and Economic Order* (Chicago: Henry Regnery, 1948), 77–91; Friedrich A. Hayek, "Economics and Knowledge," *Economica* 4 (1937): 33–54, reproduced in Hayek, *Individualism and Economic Order*, 33–56.

7. The weekly wage in the private sector is $1,202 in California and $717 in Mississippi. See Bureau of Labor Statistics, "Quarterly Census of Employment and Wages: Private, Total, All Industries, All States and US; 2016 Annual Averages, All Establishment Sizes," accessed November 22, 2017.

8. 42 Cong. Rec. H3234 (May 9, 1872) (statement of Rep. Cox), quoted in Irwin, *Clashing over Commerce*, 245.

9. Quoted in Naushad Forbes and David Wield, *From Followers to Leaders: Managing Technology and Innovation* (London: Routledge, 2002), 5.

10. "Why Farmers Are Anxious about NAFTA," *Economist*, June 29, 2017.

11. Hufbauer, Cimino, and Moran, "NAFTA at 20," 18.

12. Irwin, *Free Trade under Fire*, 288.

13. International Trade Administration, *Benefits of Trade Agreements*, 2015 (updated July 2016).

14. Irwin, *Free Trade under Fire*, 290.

15. Hufbauer, Cimino, and Moran, "NAFTA at 20," 2.

16. See United States International Trade Commission, *Economic Impact of Trade Agreements*, 255–61. See also Lorenzo Caliendo and Fernando Parro, "Estimates of the Trade and Welfare Effects of NAFTA," *Review of Economic Studies* 82 (2015): 1–44. This article evaluates the change in "welfare" as the sum of the change in terms of trade, the change in the volume of trade, and the change in real wages. The model finds that the United States gains 0.08 percent in welfare. The model calculates only the effect of tariff reductions, excluding the impact of other measures in the agreement. "Unquestionably, NAFTA had more provisions than only reducing tariff between members," the authors warn, "and by no means our results should be interpreted as the trade and welfare effects of the entire agreement" (29). The model does not include the technological change that might have been boosted by NAFTA, or NAFTA's consequences for the rate of economic growth.

17. See Hufbauer, Cimino, and Moran, "NAFTA at 20," 16; Caliendo and Parro, "Estimates of the Trade and Welfare Effects of NAFTA."

18. M. Angeles Villarreal and Ian F. Fergusson, *The North American Free Trade Agreement (NAFTA)*, Congressional Research Service, April 16, 2015, Summary.

19. US International Trade Commission, *Economic Impact of Trade Agreements*, 260. However, any plurilateral trade agreement—as opposed to truly multilateral ones such as international rules under the WTO—is likely to create *some* trade diversion. For example, flat-screen TVs imported into the United States from Mexico would probably be imported from Asia were it not for NAFTA's discrimination in favor of Mexican imports; see Robbie Whelan and Santiago Pérez, "Why Your Flat-Screen TV Would Cost More If Nafta Ends," *Wall Street Journal*, November 22, 2017. Moreover, if the demise of NAFTA were to lead to retaliation, any benefit in terms of ending trade diversion could be more than canceled.

20. This is calculated using figures from the Bureau of Economic Analysis.

21. At least, that was the case in 2011 and 2013, and there was a balance of zero in 2014, the last date in the series. See Congressional Research Service, *The North American Free Trade Agreement (NAFTA)*, April 2015, 11–12.

22. Congressional Research Service, *The North American Free Trade Agreement (NAFTA)*, 30.

8. Objection: Free Trade Is Not Fair

1. Paul Krugman makes this argument in "What Should Trade Negotiators Negotiate About?" I raise some questions about this issue in a blog post, "Taking Comparative Advantage Seriously," *EconLog*, November 17, 2017.

2. Pierre Lemieux, "Protectionism by Any Other Name," *Regulation* 37, no. 3 (2014): 5–7.

3. See Benjamin Powell, *Out of Poverty: Sweatshops in the Global Economy* (Cambridge, UK: Cambridge University Press, 2014). This book is reviewed in Pierre Lemieux, "Defending Sweatshops," *Regulation* 38, no. 2 (2015): 66–68.

4. Joan Robinson, *Economic Philosophy* (London: C.A. Watts, 1962), 45.

5. Taussig, *Tariff History of the United States*, 364. Taussig is quoting the Republican Party's 1908 platform.

6. A good summary can be found in Fernando R. Tesón, "Why Free Trade Is Required by Justice," *Social Philosophy and Policy* 29, no. 1 (2011): 126–53. Tesón states that "the redistribution of wealth resulting from protectionist laws cannot possibly be supported by moral reasons" (140).

7. Robert Nozick, *Anarchy, State, and Utopia* (New York: Basic Books, 1974), 163.

8. George Fitzhugh, *Sociology for the South or the Failure of Free Society* (London: Forgotten Books, 2015 [1854]), 170.

9. John R. Hicks, "The Pursuit of Economic Freedom," in *What We Defend: Essays in Freedom by Members of the University of Manchester*, ed. E. F. Jacob (Oxford: Oxford University Press, 1942), 112–13. See also Tyler Cowen, "A Profession with an Egalitarian Core," *New York Times*, March 16, 2013.

10. See Friedrich A. Hayek, *The Constitution of Liberty* (Chicago: University of Chicago Press, 1960); Hayek, *The Fatal Conceit: The Errors of Socialism* (Chicago: University of Chicago Press, 1988), notably chapter 3.

11. All data are for 2016. See Bureau of Economic Analysis, "International Transactions," tables 1.2 and 1.3, June 20, 2017.

12. Adding the Chinese-produced inputs in American production processes does not change these figures significantly; see Galina Hale and Bart Hobijn, "The U.S. Content of 'Made in China,'" FRBSF Economic Letter, Federal Reserve Bank of San Francisco, August 8, 2011.

13. Bureau of Labor Statistics, CPI—All Urban Consumers (Current Series), extracted on August 3, 2017.

Conclusion

1. Thomas H. Farrer, *Free Trade v. Fair Trade*, 3rd ed. (London: Free Trade Union, 1904 [1886]), 1.

2. Irwin, *Against the Tide*, 226.

Index

Figures and tables are noted by *f* and *t* following page numbers; n indicates a note.

absolute advantage, 8-11, 15, 17
Acemoglu, Daron, 55-56
agricultural goods
  exports (1980-2014), *19f*
  NAFTA and, 82, 84, 87
  supply chains, 82
  US comparative advantage, 20
Amazon, 60, 111n22
Andersen, Lill, 60
apparel industry. *See* textile
  manufacturing
Autor, David, 55-58, 65-66

Babula, Ronald, 60
balance of international payments,
  33-36
balance of trade. *See* trade
  balance
Balassa, Béla, 15
Bangladesh
  manufacturing, 57
  trade with US, 17
  wages, 7
Bernard, Andrew B., 48
Bhadwati, Jagdish, 22-23
Boeing, supply chain, 18
budget deficits, 35-36, 42

California
  domestic trade, 80
  wages, 80, 114n7
Canada. *See* North American Free
  Trade Agreement
capital services, 32
China
  exports, growth in, 55-56
  imports, 26
  subsidies, 27
  supply chains, 18, 28
  wages, 57-58, 70
China, US trade with
  benefits to US consumers, 95-97
  supply chain, 96-97
  tariffs, 3, 63
  US consumption expenditures, *96f*
  US job loss and, 65
  US trade deficit, 95
"China shock," 55-58, 65
Cobden, Richard, 101-102
collective action, theory of, 77-78
comparative advantage
  absolute advantage and, 8-11, 15, 17
  agricultural goods, 20
  beneficial trade and, 13
  defined, 17

comparative advantage (*continued*)
  fairness and, 90
  manufacturing, 47
  NAFTA, 87
  real wages and, 70–71
  shift in, 47
  supply chains and, 17–20
  theory of, 10–16, 70, 104n5
  US, 19–20, 47–48
competition, against low-cost foreign
    producers, 7–16
  absolute and comparative advantage,
    8–9
  comparative advantage, theory of,
    10–16
  fairness and, 90–91
competition, domestic, 71–72
concessions, 22–23
Congressional Research Service, 85
Constitution, US, 104n10
consumer price index (CPI), 97
consumers
  Chinese-made goods, 95–97, *96f*
  deadweight loss, 25
  import tariffs increasing prices for, 78
  income, and consumption of
    internationally traded goods, 67
  jobs *vs.* consumption, 53–54
  trade benefits for, xii, 67–68, 69, 87,
    95–97
Corn Law Controversy, 101–102
Cox, Samuel, 80–81
CPI (consumer price index), 97
current account, 32–36, 39–40, *40t*

deadweight loss, 25–26, 27
Devaraj, Srikant, 57
developed countries
  labor market polarization, 74
  manufacturing transformation,
    46–47
developing countries
  comparative advantage, 47
  manufacturing, 46–47
  trade and economic growth, 60–61

wages, 7
WTO rules, 84
Dollar, David, 48
domestic producers
  deadweight loss, 25
  domestic competition, 71–72
  import of intermediate inputs, 28
domestic trade
  domestic competition, 71–72
  politics of, 79–81
Dorn, David, 55–56, 57–58
duties. *See* export taxes; tariffs

earnings. *See* wages
economic growth
  jobs and, 63–68
  protectionism and, 59
  trade and, 58–65, 99
Economist, 28, 34, 48
education level, wages and, 74–75, *74f,*
    113n7
employment. *See* jobs; unemployment
    rate
ethics. *See* moral concerns
European Union, imports, 26
exchange rate, 33, 40, 42
export subsidies. *See* subsidies
export taxes, prohibition on, 104n10
exports
  as costs of trade, 21, 22–23
  prohibitions on, 37, 107n12
  US, *19f, 40t, 41f*

factories. *See* manufacturing
fairness
  comparative advantage and, 90
  free trade and, 89–94
  free trade as, xi, 92, 94, 99
  liberty and, 92, 93–94, 100
  moral concerns, 89–94
  protectionism and, 92–93
  subsidies and, 90
  tariffs and, 90
Fajhelbaum, Pablo, 67
Farrer, Thomas, 101–102

federal debt, 35–36
federal deficits, 35–36, 42
financial account, 33–35, 39–40, *40t*
Fitzhugh, George, 92
foreign exchange rate, 33, 40, 42
foreign investment, 33–36
  balance of international payments,
    33–36
  benefits of, 38
  as driver of trade deficit, x
  federal deficits and, 42
  financial account, 39–40
France
  manufacturing, 46, 48
  supply chain, 18
free trade
  cost-benefit analysis, 21, 25–26,
    99–100
  defined, 2–4
  economists' consensus concerning, 1–2
  exports as costs, 21, 22–23
  as fair trade, xi, 92, 94, 99
  fears of, 1
  GDP and, 63–65, *64f*
  harmfulness argument, 21–28
  as immigration substitute, 81
  imports as benefits of, 21, 22–23
  labor productivity and, 70, 73
  liberty and, 93–94, 100
  moral concerns about, xiii–xv, 89–92,
    92–94
  national sovereignty and, 93–94
  net benefits of, 23–28
  reducing government power, 101
  as unfair, 89–94
  unilateral free trade, 36–38
  wages and, 70, 73
  See also trade
free trade agreements (FTAs), xiii,
  83–87, 101
  See also North American Free Trade
    Agreement

Gallup's "State of the American
  Workplace" survey, 54

GDP
  exports and, *41f*
  import tariffs and, 63–65, *65f*
  imports and, x, 29–30, *41f*
  manufacturing's contribution to, 46
  NAFTA and, 86, *86f*
  per capita, 50, *50f*
  trade and, 18, 63–65, *65f*
  US, 26, *41f*
geographical distance, 14
goods and services balance. *See* trade
  balance
Great Recession. *See* recession
  (2008-2009)
"Great Society," 93
Griswold, Daniel, 108n14, 112n34

Hanson, Gordon, 55–56, 57–58
Harmonized Tariff Schedule of the
  United States, 3
Hayek, F. A., 79, 93
Heckscher, Eli, 70–71, 112n2
Hicks, John, 93
Hicks, Michael, 56–57
Horn Welch, Karen, 60, 61

immigration, free trade as substitute
  for, 81
import quotas, 3, 78
import substitution, 61, 111n30
import tariffs. *See* tariffs
imports
  as benefits of trade, x, 21, 22–23
  by country, 26
  GDP and, x, 29–30, *41f*
  of manufactured goods, 45
  US, 26, *40t, 41f*
income. *See* wages
income, per capita, 17–18, 50
income distribution, 15, 70–71
India, protectionism, 81
"infant industry" argument, 59
An Inquiry into the Nature and
  Causes of the Wealth of Nations
  (Smith), 8

internal costs, 9, 10, 12-13
International Monetary Fund, 17-18
international payments, 33-36, 38, 39, 40t
international trade. See free trade; trade
Irwin, Douglas, 79, 102

Japan
   manufacturing, 46, 58
   supply chain, 18
   technological progress and job growth, 55
jobs
   vs. consumption, 53-54
   economic growth and, 63-68
   gained from technology, 55, 57
   gained from trade, 63-65
   labor market polarization, 74-75
   labor mobility, 56, 57
   lost to efficiency, xi-xii
   lost to protectionism, 63
   lost to reclassification, 47
   lost to technology, xii, 46-48, 54-57, 99
   lost to trade, 53-62, 65
   manufacturing sector, 45, 46-47, 49, 50f, 51, 56-57, 99, 108n4, 108n6
   noneconomic aspects, 54
   population growth and, 65-67, 66f
   purpose of, 53-54, 61
   separations and new hires, 112n34
   total civilian employment, 49, 50f, 110n13
   See also unemployment rate
Jones Act (1920), 3

Khandelwal, Amit, 67
Klein, Daniel, 2
knowledge problem, 79
Korea, supply chain, 18
Krugman, Paul, 2, 11, 36, 61

labor mobility, 56, 57
labor productivity. See productivity
less developed countries (LDCs). See developing countries

liberty, free trade, fairness, and, 92, 93-94, 100
Lipsey, Robert E., 42
lobbying. See politics of trade
low-cost foreign producers, competition against, 7-16
   absolute and comparative advantage, 8-9
   theory of comparative advantage, 10-16
   wages, 7
low-income consumers. See poor people

Mad about Trade (Griswold), 108n14
Manchester Liberals, 93
manufacturing
   change in, 45-47
   "China shock," 55-56
   comparative advantage, shift in, 47-48
   efficiency, xi-xii
   GDP and, 46
   loss of, 45-49, 50f, 51, 55-57, 65, 108n4
   new manufacturing and US economy, 49-52, 99
   production increases, 46, 51-52, 52f
   supply chains, 46-47
   US comparative advantage, 20
   US exports (1980-2014), 19f
   value added, 51-52
"market failures," 79
McKinsey Global Institute, 57
mercantilism, 1, 7-8, 22, 31
merchandise (goods) balance, 32, 39, 40t, 41-42, 41f
methodological individualism, 28
Mexico
   supply chain, 19, 28
   US, trade with, 16
   wages, 7, 16, 70
   See also North American Free Trade Agreement
Mill, James, 22, 104n5

Milliken & Company of Spartanburg,
   South Carolina, 20
Mississippi
   domestic trade, 80
   wages, 80, 114n7
moral concerns
   fairness, 89–94
   of free trade, xiii–xv, 89–92, 92–94
   of protectionism, xiii–xv, 92–93
Most-Favored Nation requirement, 83
Mulligan, Casey, 54

NAFTA. See North American Free Trade
   Agreement
national debt, 35–36
national sovereignty, free trade and,
   93–94
nationalist ideology, protectionism and,
   81, 89
Nehru, Jawaharlal, 81
new manufacturing, 49–52
North American Free Trade Agreement
   (NAFTA), 83–87
   agricultural goods, 82, 84, 87
   arguments against, xii–xiii
   benefits of, 84, 87, 101, 114n16
   comparative advantage, 87
   GDP and, 86, 86f
   impact of abolition of, 84, 85f,
      115n19
   import tariffs and, 84, 85f, 114n16
   increasing trade, 85–86
   merchandise deficit, 86f, 87
   rules, 3
   supply chains, 84, 87
   US economy and, 85
   US exports, 95
Nozick, Robert, 92

Obama, Barack, 63
offshoring, 57
Ohlin, Bertil, 70–71, 112n2
oil exports, prohibition on, 37
opportunity costs, 12
optimal tariff argument, 26–28

pauper labor argument, 69
Philippines, wage rates and
   productivity, 70
plurilateral trade agreements, 115n19
politics of trade, 77–82
   domestic and international trade,
      79–81
   new business interests, 82
   protectionism, 77–79
   sugar lobby, 78
poor people
   sweatshops, 90–91
   trade benefits for, xii, 67–68, 91
population growth, jobs and, 65–67,
   66f
Powell, John, vii
Price, Brendan, 55–56
price ratio, 12
productivity
   as employment-augmenting,
      54–55
   factors contributing to, 15–16
   free trade and, 70, 73
   manufacturing sector, 46, 51–52, 52f
   rich countries, 15–16
   wages and, 70, 73–75, 73f, 113n6
protectionism
   abolition, recommendations for,
      100–101
   as coercive redistribution, 80, 102
   dampening economic growth, 59
   as defense against "market failures," 79
   as directed against nationals, 102
   export prohibitions, 37
   fairness and, 92–93
   harm from, 100
   "infant industry" argument, 59
   job loss from, 63
   as Luddite resistance to change, 48
   morality of, xiii–xv, 92–93
   nationalist ideology and, 81, 89
   politics of, 77–79
   reducing productivity, 59
   Republican Party, 91
   retaliatory, 37

protectionism (*continued*)
  special interests and, 77–78, 91
  steel industry, 59, 78–79
  sugar industry, 78
public debt, 35–36

Ramaswamy, Ramana, 108n4
real wages, 69, 70–72
recession (2008-2009)
  labor market depression, 54
  manufacturing production, 51
  NAFTA merchandise deficit, 87
  recovery from, 43–44, 46, 51, 52
Republican Party, protectionism, 91
retailers, opposition to trade
  restrictions, 82
Ricardo, David, 8, 13
Robinson, Joan, 37, 91
Ross, Wilbur, 29, 31
Rothwell, Jonathan, 56
Rowthorn, Robert, 108n4

Salomons, Anna, 55, 65–66
Samuelson, Paul A., 112n3
Sarkar, Prabirjit, 60
Say's law, 66
Senior, Nassau, 58
service sector, US
  comparative advantage, 19–20
  exports, *19f*, 20
  in factories, 47
  international transactions (2016),
    40t
  trade balance and, 32, 39, 95–96
Smeets, Valerie, 48
Smith, Adam, 8, 59
steel industry, 3, 59, 78–79
Stolper, Wolfgang F., 112n3
subsidies, 26, 27, 90
sugar industry, 3, 78
supply chains
  agricultural goods, 82
  comparative advantage and, 14, 17–20
  complex goods, 14, 28
  international integration, xi, 28

manufacturing productivity and,
  46–47
NAFTA, 84, 87
sweatshop argument, 90–91
Sweden
  manufacturing, 46
supply chain, 18

tariffs
  Chinese tires, 63
  fairness and, 90
  GDP and, 63–65, *64f*
  increasing domestic price of goods,
    24, 78
  introduction, 3
  Most-Favored Nation requirement, 83
  NAFTA, 84, *85f*, 114n16
  net loss from, 24, 25–26
  optimal tariff argument, 26–28
  rates, 3
  redistribution effects, 24–25
Taussig, Frank, 78, 91
technology
  labor market polarization and, 75
  manufacturing job loss and, xii,
    46–48, 54–57, 99
  net increase in jobs by, xii, 54–55
terms of trade, 12, 27, 41–42
terms-of-trade argument, 26–28
Tesón, Fernando R., 115n6
textile manufacturing, 20, 59, 97, 107n12
Thailand
  manufacturing, 57
  wages, 7
tire industry, 63
Torrens, Robert, 104n5
TPP (Trans-Pacific Partnership), 3
trade
  benefits to consumers, xii, 67–68, 69,
    87, 95–97
  benefits to countries, 71
  benefits to domestic competition,
    71–72
  benefits to importers and exporters, 71
  benefits to poor, xii, 67–68, 91

economic growth fostered by,
58–65, 99
income distribution and, 70–71
increase in, under NAFTA, 85–86
increase in (1960–2015), 18
increasing income, 17–18
job growth from, 63–65
jobs, long-term and dynamic benefits,
58–61
jobs, net jobs, 54–55
jobs, short-run costs, 55–58
jobs *vs.* consumption, 53–54
politics of, 77–82
as production technique, 11
wages and, 69–72
See also free trade
trade agreements
free trade agreements, xiii, 83–87, 101
impact of, 68
plurilateral, 115n19
trade diversion and, 115n19
See also North American Free Trade
Agreement
trade balance, 39–44
balance of goods, 32, 39
balance of services, 32, 39
defined, 31, 39
England (1700s), vii, 7–8
factors in, 34
US, 32, 39, *40t*, 41–42
trade deficit, US
argument against, 31–38
balance of international payments,
33–36
benefits of, 38
with China, 95
current deficit, 32, 39, 95
defined, 32
drivers of, x
GDP and, 29, 31, 41
history, 32, 41–42
unemployment rate and, 43–44, *43f*,
108n14
trade diversion, 86, 115n19
trade negotiations, 22–23

trade restrictions, 3
trade surplus, US
agricultural sector, 20
defined, 32
GDP and, 29
history, 32
service sector, 20
unemployment rate and, 43–44, *43f*
Trans-Pacific Partnership (TPP), 3

unemployment rate, 43–44, *43f*, 108n14
See also jobs
unilateral free trade, case for, 36–38
United Kingdom
export prohibitions, 107n12
manufacturing, 46
postwar economy, 15
supply chain, 18
unilateral free trade, 36
United States
agriculture trade surplus, 20
Bangladesh, trade with, 17
comparative advantage, 19–20, 47–48
exports, *19f, 40t, 41f*
free trade agreements, 83
imports, as percentage of total world
imports, 26
labor market polarization, 74–75
manufacturing jobs, 45, 46–48, 55–57,
108n6
manufacturing wages, 16
Mexico, trade with, 16
Net International Investment Position,
33–34
as percentage of total world GDP, 26
postwar economy, 15
service sector, 19–20
supply chain, 18–19, 28
technological progress and job
growth, 55
Vietnam, trade with, 16
See also China, US trade with; North
American Free Trade Agreement;
specific topics
US International Trade Commission, 68

value judgments, 89
Vietnam
  manufacturing, 57
  trade, 16
  wages, 7

Wacziarg, Romain, 60, 61
wages
  comparative advantage and,
    70–71
  developing countries, 7
  education and, 74–75, *74f*
  factors of production and, 112n3
  productivity and, 70, 73–75, *73f*,
    113n6

  real wages, 69, 70–72
  trade and, 69–72
Wall Street Journal, 29
Warzynski, Frederic, 48
welfare (economics)
  defined, 109n1, 114n16
  indicators of, 53–54, 61
welfare (government assistance), 56
work. *See* jobs
World Bank, 17–18
World Trade Organization (WTO)
  benefits of, 101
  free trade agreements, 83, 84
  rules, xiii, 3
  on trade and per capita income, 17–18

About the Author

Professor Pierre Lemieux is an economist affiliated with the Department of Management Sciences of the University of Quebec in Outaouais. He has lectured at several universities in Canada and served as a consultant for a number of private and public organizations. Lemieux has written books on economics, public policy, and political philosophy, and he has been published in the *Wall Street Journal,* Canada's *Financial Post,* and France's *Figaro Économie.*